Experimental Designs
in
Sociological Research

Experimental Designs
in
Sociological Research

By

F. STUART CHAPIN

Chairman, Department of Sociology
Director, School of Social Work
University of Minnesota

Harper & Brothers Publishers
New York   *London*

EXPERIMENTAL DESIGNS IN
SOCIOLOGICAL RESEARCH

Copyright, 1947, by Harper & Brothers
Printed in the United States of America

CONTENTS

INTRODUCTION

AMONG the problems of human relations that concern us today and demand attention there are a few which have been studied by experimental methods, not in the laboratory or yet in the formal classroom situation, but right out in the natural community. What can we learn from these experiments about the possibility of an affirmative answer to such pressing questions as: Can juvenile delinquency be treated to diminish it, or to prevent its recurrence? Does healthful housing in public projects lead to improved individual and social adjustment of the members of low-income families? Is the morale of needy persons aided by a work program superior to the morale of those who receive only poor relief? Can successful adjustment to our increasingly complex environment be achieved by formal school education or student counseling programs?

The experimental studies described and analyzed in this book seek the beginnings of answers to these questions. Since each study is a single experiment, as yet not repeated, the results do not reveal any dramatic or spectacular achievements any more than a single experiment in physical science solves a problem. Nor can we generalize to the community as a whole from the results of any one of these experiments. But it does seem evident that the results are sufficiently favorable and objective to hold forth the promise of at least subsequent success, if only sufficient determination and patience can be exercised in repeating these experiments until we discover the way to verification. The needed next steps are to repeat them in the study of the same type of problem elsewhere but under like conditions. It is with the hope that this will be done that the present book has been written. As illustrated in these studies, the newly developed research methods of experimental design, applied in the community situation, seem to point the way by which we can overcome, in the course of time, some of the complexities of social interaction that have hitherto baffled rational and objective description of certain acute problems of human relations. At the same time that this optimistic note is expressed, a word of warning should also be recorded, namely, that progress with this method of experimental design may be slow and will undoubtedly require a considerable span of time and numbers of repetitions of an experiment before the stage of reliable generalization and dependable prediction can be attained.

Programs to prevent the recurrence of social ills always rest upon the assumption that social cause and effect sequences are known, whether or not this assumption is implicit or explicitly stated in the program. More research in this area is needed to implement social planning and social action programs. The use of the method of experimental design to discover and to expose the causal complexes in the social situation of a given period has just begun to claim the attention of research workers in human relations.

My own interest in the possibility of an adaptation of the experimental method of physical science to the study of the problems of human relationship dates from 1916, and my first published papers on this subject appeared in the *Scientific Monthly* of February and March, 1917. Since then some development has been recorded in our knowledge of how to use experimental designs as a method of sociological research. Thus the present book is an account of nine experimental studies over a period of years by my students, Helen Christiansen, Nathan Mandel, Julius A. Jahn, John N. Burrus, T. E. Kyllonen, and Marvin Taves, done under my direction, and also an account of several comparable studies by Naomi Barer, Stuart C. Dodd, Reuben Hill, and Harry M. Shulman.

The criterion of selection for analysis of these studies in experimental design is the condition that they be set up in the normal community situation. Numerous studies of an experimental kind which are located in the schoolroom situation or in some approximation to a laboratory situation have been described in the literature of social psychology and educational psychology. It has sometimes been contended that the use of experimental designs in sociological research is limited by our inability to establish controls outside of the schoolroom or laboratory situations. For these reasons we exclude from this book the experimental studies done in classroom or approximate laboratory situations, believing that these have been described elsewhere in accessible publications,[1] and focus our attention on nine studies conducted in the normal community situation. The assumption is that it is worth while to analyze the limitations on experimental study set by community situations in the hope that thereby the way may be pointed to devices that can be used to overcome these limitations. Two of the nine studies stem from the school environment or a semi-laboratory situation, but since their validity is tested largely in terms of wider community effects, we regard them as meeting the essential criterion just laid down. They are the studies of Hill, on student adjustment on the campus of the University of Wisconsin, and Shulman, on the treatment of juvenile delinquency in New York, in which the classroom situation is a contributory factor in social treatment.

The purpose of this little book is to illustrate the method of experimental design by reproducing concrete studies, and is not to offer an extensive and critical examination of the literature. That task was well done by Ernest Greenwood in his *Experimental Sociology,* 1945. This book and Greenwood's are, therefore, complementary, since his book is in the nature of a theoretical discussion of the fundamental logic of experimental designs, whereas mine is in the nature of a source book of examples of specific application analyzed in some detail.

There appear to be three main types of experimental design applied to the study of problems in the natural community situation: (1) a cross-sectional design which makes controlled observations for a single date; (2) a projected design of "before" and "after" study, in which an attempt is made to measure the effects at some future date of the social forces set in motion by some method of social treatment or by a social program, thus following through the flow of events from a present date to some future date; and (3) what we

---

[1] This condition excludes such interesting social experiments as those of Lewin and Lippitt, but these have been described in detail in accessible literature and need no further analysis here.

have called an ex post facto design, in which some present effect is traced backward to an assumed causal complex of factors or forces operating at a prior date, using for this purpose such records as are available, since no new measures of the past can be made in the present. The organization of subject matter follows the order of these patterns of experimental design.

ACKNOWLEDGMENTS

For permission to reproduce in whole or in part, as sections of this book, certain articles previously published by the author, acknowledgments are due the editors of the *American Journal of Sociology*, the *American Sociological Review,* the *Scientific Monthly, Social Forces,* and *Sociometry*. The continued aid and interest of my wife, Eula P. Chapin, has been an ever-present source of encouragement.

Any errors that inadvertently appear in the summaries of the experimental studies of Naomi Barer, Stuart C. Dodd, Reuben Hill, and Harry M. Shulman are the responsibility of the author.

F. STUART CHAPIN

Experimental Designs
in
Sociological Research

Chapter I

NATURAL SOCIAL EXPERIMENTS
BY TRIAL AND ERROR

THE THEORY AND PRACTICE OF THE EXPERIMENTAL METHOD [1]

SINCE the time of Comte, sociologists have been searching for a method to apply to the data of society which would yield as positive results as those attained in the realm of physical science. The experimental method has contributed in large measure to the striking achievements of modern science. This method allows us to analyze out relations of cause and effect more rapidly and clearly than by other methods. It permits verification by many observers. It has substituted for unreasonable prejudice a definite sort of proof that has attained sufficient certainty to justify prediction.

Experiment is simply observation under controlled conditions. When observation alone fails to disclose the factors that operate in a given problem, it is necessary for the scientist to resort to experiment. The line between observation and experiment is not a sharp one. Observation tends gradually to take on the character of an experiment. Experiment may be considered to have begun when there is actual human interference with the conditions that determine the phenomenon under observation.

The fundamental rule of the experimental method is to vary only one condition at a time and to maintain all other conditions rigidly constant. There are two good reasons for this procedure: In the first place, if two conditions are varied at one time and an effect is produced, it is not possible to tell which condition is responsible, or whether both have acted jointly; in the second place, when no effect ensues, how can we tell which condition is responsible, or whether one has neutralized the other?

---

[1] Much of this chapter appeared originally in an article, "The Experimental Method and Sociology," in the *Scientific Monthly* of February and March, 1917.

Specific illustrations from the fields of physics and botany may serve to bring the principle to mind. Newton desired to prove the "equal gravitation of all substances." Since the resistance of the air to pendulums of different bulk and shape varied, it was necessary to reduce this condition to a constant factor before the single force of gravitation could be observed. The desired end was accomplished by the construction of hollow pendulums of equal boxes of wood and of identical outward size and shape, hung by equal threads, with centers of oscillation at equal distances from the points of suspension. When these wooden pendulums were filled with equal weights of different substances and vibrated with equal velocity, any subsequent inequality in observed vibration of two pendulums must rise from the only condition which was different, namely, the chemical composition of the substances in the pendulums. Since no inequality was observed, it was concluded that the chemical composition of substances had no appreciable influence upon the force of gravitation.

The botanist endeavors to discover the effects of light upon plant growth and resorts to the experimental method. A glass bell jar is placed over a plant and the growth compared with a plant in a shaded bell jar and another plant without a bell jar. But since the sun heats up one bell jar and the resultant warmth affects growth, it is necessary to shield the jar from the direct rays of the sun. In this way it is possible to exert a considerable degree of control over certain conditions which affect growth.

Natural Experiments

Comte conceived of pathological cases as indirect social experiments. Whenever the regular course of a phenomenon is interfered with in any determinate manner, true experimentation takes place, and hence according to this interpretation of experimentation it is not important to have a conscious agent to effect the change. While it may be stated at once that Comte's notion of experimentation in the realm of living things was based upon the limited biological knowledge of his time, his concept of social experiments caused by the action of natural forces upon society has been of considerable suggestiveness for sociology. Under certain natural circumstances physical factors at the basis of social life have been limited, or held constant, or the ordinary restraining factors have been removed so that the sociologist need only observe the effects.

Such a natural experiment exists in the Arctic Circle where the Eskimos live an isolated life under conditions of extreme simplicity. Here nature has withdrawn her usual variety of resources in flora and fauna, she has produced a pretty constant color scheme (or rather absence of color), controlled her temperature scale in such a fashion that variation in flora and fauna is repressed, and accomplished the maximum degree of isolation from the rest of mankind. Under these circumstances the struggle for existence is severely simple and the inhabitants have evolved a remarkable system of adapted ways. The Eskimos, in the course of adapting their architectural methods to the only material at hand—snow—have developed the dome, a most unusual form among primitive peoples. Civilized man cannot better this snow igloo of the Eskimo and finds it necessary to adopt other Eskimo ways in the Arctic region. Other adaptations appear in the form of bone snow spectacles, bone bows, and skiffs made of skins. In social life adaptations are seen in the absence of commercialism (due to isolation and lack of surplus), the elementary organization of property, the institution of polygamy (due to the high male death rate), and the custom of patricide (due to scarcity of food). Here the sociologist may observe the effects upon social life of the elimination of many physical conditions considered fundamental in temperate climes.

Nature has performed an interesting experiment in the effects of isolation upon a people at a much higher cultural stage. In the southern Appalachian Mountains there live over a million people who are the direct descendants of the colonial population of America. In these isolated valleys remote from the swarming centers of population they have clung fast to the colonial culture with its spinning wheel and cumbersome hand loom. New ideas, modern inventions, contemporary science have come to revolutionize the life of the rest of the nation, while these quiet folk, serene in their simplicity, have been oblivious to all the rush and worry of new problems. President Frost, of Berea College, called them "our contemporary ancestors of the South," and they do indeed reproduce the life of colonial times, constituting a natural experiment in the effects of isolation.

EXPERIMENTATION UPON HUMAN BEINGS

But the sociologist cannot rely on natural experiments alone to test his hypotheses. Such experiments are infrequent, are not easy to recognize, are difficult to observe properly, and will probably become more and more infrequent as time goes on because of the standardizing effects of the spread of a more homogeneous culture over the world.

Have direct experiments ever been performed on groups of human beings by human beings? Have certain circumstances of social life ever been controlled or limited by conscious human interference? These questions have both a historical and a contemporary answer.

It may be stated as a truism that just as soon as the sociologist passes from the method of passive observation to active interference with the determining conditions of a social problem he begins to encounter a stiffening resistance. The social reformer meets objections and obstacles at every step. All sorts of opposition are met by advocates of minimum wage bills, eugenic marriage laws, compulsory vaccination, and child labor bills. The people believe that serious questions of individual rights, personal freedom, and moral responsibility are involved. It is felt that, while the subject of experiment in physical science is inert and insensitive matter, in the social field the experimenter is dealing with exceedingly complex units capable of great individual suffering if the experiment should go wrong. There is a popular disposition to withhold or question the sanction for an act which puts in the hands of one person, or of a group, an apparently arbitrary control over the welfare and destiny of other assumedly equal human beings. Ideals of individual freedom and the sanctity of human life have been won after generations of struggle and are regarded as too precious a heritage to abrogate in instances where the outcome is doubtful. The parent who experimented upon his children by limiting their food, strangely clothing them, or keeping them from school and intercourse with other human beings would soon be investigated and perhaps brought to court by the agent of a children's protective society. Certain acts although practiced in a spirit of scientific experimentation are nevertheless considered criminal and their authors prosecuted by agencies which seek to preserve social welfare. One may experiment upon plants or insects without encountering moral objections, but just as soon as human life is experimented upon, society reacts unfavorably, either through its unorganized method of public opinion or through its more systematized agencies.

The line between permissible and forbidden subjects of experimentation is not sharply drawn. Even for worthy scientific ends, when it affects the lives of higher animals, experimentation is censured. In fact, there is now systematic opposition in the form of an organization of anti-vivisectionists. Yet the experimental method has nowhere made more positive contributions to human welfare than in the field of live animal experimentation. The death rate from diphtheria has been reduced by the use of antitoxin. Careful experimentation upon animals has given us the anti-meningitis serum which has reduced child mortality from this distressing disease. Experimentation upon dogs has given us the beneficient thyroid treatment for cretinism in children. Inoculation against malaria and bone grafting have been made possible by animal experimentation.[2] No harm has been done to social ideals and precious human life has been saved.

Yet in spite of this splendid array of worthy achievements which have reduced the pitiful suffering of innocent little children, there are still undiscriminating individuals who see in all animal experimentation a great moral menace. Such has been the mistaken zeal of these persons, in the belief that their efforts are protecting our moral standards, that legitimate and beneficent researches of medical scientists have been hampered.

But where draw the line between experiments on living things and experiments upon human beings? Certainly these cases of

<hr>

[2] H. D. Chapin, "What Animal Experimentation Has Done for Children," *Popular Science Monthly*, January, 1915, pp. 55–62.

animal experimentation are on the border line of moral standards. They form very illuminating illustrations of sincere differences of opinion as to where the end may and may not justify the means. Cases of the "poison squad" method of the military scientists or of other instances in which human individuals voluntarily renounce certain rights and freely submit to experimentation would seem to grade off into this intermediate region where in connection with live animal experimentation the usual moral standards of the sanctity of life are observed to be border line and uncertain. As a matter of fact, there seems to be a regular evolutionary series of stages in the development of the sanction for experimentation. These stages are related to the character of the subject. The sanction for experimentation on inanimate matter and on plant life is within the personal choice of the scientist; no one questions his right. But just as soon as animal experimentation is reached, particularly in the case of higher animals capable of considerable suffering, the sanction of personal choice is regarded by many people as inadequate. And when human life is reached all people demand that a higher sanction for the act than personal will be obtained.

When individuals freely renounce certain rights and for the benefit of humanity submit to experimentation, society does not feel serious concern and may even recognize their self-sacrifice and heroism. The state alone, of human agencies, seems to possess by common consent the social sanction for mandatory interference with the normal lives of persons. Unless the individual voluntarily renounces his personal rights, none but the state may morally and legally take them from him. Society is the only official sociological experimenter. In the past, the sovereign power over human life wielded by the state has more often been exercised by an aristocratic or plutocratic minority than voluntarily and legally delegated by the people to their chosen representatives or executives. History is replete with illustrations of this fact. Tyrannical governments have experimented endlessly and thoughtlessly with the lives and welfare of the people. It is only in recent times that a democratic organization of governments has permitted some people to control legislative experiments upon human life and social welfare.

The Utopian Community Experiments

But before considering those social experiments sanctioned and attempted by the state, and always characterized by a certain amount of constraint, it will be well to examine a few cases of local community experimentation in which the elements are simple and the results positive.

The associationists of the early nineteenth century, Owen and Fourier, advocated the establishment of communities organized on a more ideal basis than the society of the time and promulgated broad humanitarian plans for the regeneration of mankind.

Robert Owen was a practical and successful manufacturer and his cotton mills at New Lanark, Scotland, were models of the time for all employers who sought the welfare of their operatives as well as efficient business organization. Owen's unquestioned achievements at New Lanark brought him a world-wide reputation and convinced him of the practicability of putting ideals of social reform into everyday life. He firmly believed that "man's character is formed for him by the circumstances that surround him, that he is not a fit subject for praise or blame, and that any general character, good or bad, may be given to the world by applying means which are to a great extent under the control of human governments."[3] Assuming then that, at bottom, human nature is fundamentally good, it only remained to eliminate the restraining bonds and the demoralizing influences of existing society to attain harmonious social relations in an ideal community. Owen thought that the evils of the capitalistic system were due to the restraining effects of private property, orthodox religion, and the existing institution of marriage.[4] The remedy for present evils was, therefore, the abolition of these three institutions.

It was with full confidence that Owen embarked upon the experiment of putting into practice these social ideals. Early in 1825 he purchased 30,000 acres of fertile land of the Rappite Community at

[3] Robert Dale Owen, *Atlantic Monthly*, 1873.
[4] G. B. Lockwood, *The New Harmony Communities,* Chronicle Co., Indianapolis, 1902, p. 63.

Harmony, Indiana, and rechristened the place New Harmony. There were 3000 acres of land already under cultivation, fine orchards, 18 acres of full-bearing vines, a regularly laid out town of 160 houses with streets at right angles to one another, and a public square with large brick buildings.[5]

Founded on the principles of common ownership of property, an unorthodox religion, and a simple marriage relation, as Owen understood them, the New Harmony community of 900 souls started on what was to be an epoch-making experiment in the reconstruction of society. Back of the rich natural endowment stood Owen with his generous fortune, ready to assist. But although well supplied with material things and supported by the unfaltering enthusiasm of Owen, the community came to a disastrous end in 1827.[6] The seamy side of human nature appears to have cropped out from the beginning. The community was a very heterogeneous group of persons from many states of the Union. Petty jealousies and quarrels were the constant order of events. One observer writes:

"The people in the town continued strangers to each other, in spite of all their meetings, their balls, their frequent occasions of congregating in the hall, and all their pretence of cooperation. From the first time I set foot within this little town of one half mile square, I think there is not one within the range of my observations during my traveling in other towns of the United States, where the same number of persons, living together within such a compass for so many months, and daily and hourly passing and repassing each other, were so perfectly strangers, and void of all personal intimacy with each other's feelings, views, situations and, very generally, names." [7]

Witness to this state of affairs is borne by the local newspaper, the *Gazette,* for at one time it makes reference to the fact that "the most eccentric and violent characters" had left the community. Again it admits that "the principal thing to be contended with is the char-

[5] Macdonald's MSS Collection, quoted by W. A. Hinds, *American Communities,* Kerr & Co., Chicago, rev. ed., 1902, pp. 130–131.

[6] *Ibid.,* p. 134.

[7] Lockwood, *op. cit.,* p. 165.

acter formed by a new country. Families have been here collected without any relation to each other's views and peculiarities. Many of these persons, after their arrival, have been deprived of more or less of their property, and a general system of trading speculation exists among them, each one trying to get the best of the other. Confidence can not, therefore, exist among them, and there is an unreasonable spirit of suspicion prevalent. Inexperience in community enterprises is another great obstacle, and education alone can overcome these difficulties." [8]

In the New Harmony *Gazette* of March 28, 1827, the failure of the experiment is acknowledged in these words:

"Our own opinion is that Robert Owen ascribed too little influence to early anti-social circumstances that had surrounded many of the quickly collected inhabitants of New Harmony before their arrival here, and too much to the circumstances which experience might enable them to create around themselves in the future. He sought to abridge the period of human suffering by an immediate and decisive step, and the plan was boldly conceived; the failure would only afford proof that the conception in this particular case was not as practical as it was benevolent, in as much as the mass of the individuals at New Harmony were not prepared for so advanced a measure."

In an address at New Harmony Hall on April 13, 1828, Owen said, speaking of the failure of his experiment:

"This proves that families trained in the individual system, have not acquired those moral characteristics of forebearance and charity necessary for confidence and harmony; and communities, to be successful, must consist of persons devoid of prejudice, and possessed of moral feelings in unison with the laws of human nature." [9]

Other observers concluded that a communistic system such as Owen had devised could not exist unless in a place utterly removed from contact with the world or save with the help of some powerful religious conviction. [10]

[8] Quoted in *ibid.*, pp. 169–170.
[9] *Ibid.*, p. 214.
[10] Hinds, *op. cit.*, p. 135.

To the extent to which the institutions of private property, religion, and marriage were eliminated or controlled as constant conditions in the life of New Harmony, we have here a real social experiment. On the assumption that these three fundamental human institutions were actually eliminated or reduced to constant elements, we have experimental proof of the instability of society without them. But granting all this, general conclusions are invalidated by the fact of heterogeneity of population, a variable and uncontrolled element in the experiment. The deplorable absence of like-mindedness in New Harmony vitiates any inference as to the ultimate effect upon society of the elimination of these fundamental institutions, unless it be the conclusion that without the unifying discipline of these factors a heterogeneous aggregate of people cannot live together in peace and harmony. But this is not a new principle of sociological knowledge.

Charles Fourier (1772–1837), the contemporary of Robert Owen, was also a keen critic of the existing industrial system and placed great stress on the principle of association as a remedy for social injustice. Fourier advocated the reconstruction of society on the lines of small self-supporting cooperative communities called phalanxes. Each association was to be composed of some 1800 members who worked in harmony with one another for the benefit of the community. Every worker was to take up a different task at the end of two hours, in order that there might be the spice of variety. Labor was to be paid for in order of the necessity, usefulness, and agreeableness of the task. Fourier believed that the proposed reorganization of society would permit all who started productive work at eighteen to retire for a life of leisure at twenty-eight.

Fourier's ideas were accepted with enthusiasm by the inhabitants of Brook Farm in 1844. This interesting community was organized in 1841 by a group of New England idealists—orators, philosophers, poets, and transcendentalists. The Rev. George Ripley, founder of the Brook Farm society, proposed "to establish the external relations of life on the basis of wisdom and purity; to apply the principles of justice and love to our social organization in accordance with the laws of Divine Providence; to substitute a system of brotherly cooperation for one of selfish competition; to institute an attractive, efficient and productive system of industry; to diminish the desire of excessive accumulation by making the acquisition of individual property subservient to upright and disinterested uses; and to guarantee to each other forever the means of physical support and spiritual progress." [11]

The association was founded on a joint-stock proprietorship with capital shares of $100 each and a guaranty of 5 per cent per annum interest return. Although communism in the basic property of the community was not practiced, there were common industries, equal wages, a common guaranty of support to all members, their children, and family dependents, and housing, food, clothing, and other necessities without charge exceeding a certain amount fixed annually by the members. Education and the use of the library were free to all members. [12]

"The aim was to secure as many hours as was practicable from the necessary toil of providing for the wants of the body, that there might be more leisure to provide for the deeper wants of the soul." [13]

The testimony of observers seems to be agreed that this association of idealists lived in harmonious relations. It is said that the survivors of Brook Farm long cherished the memory of the few years spent in associative life as the happiest and most profitable they had known. [14]

The acceptance of Fourierism in 1844 appears to have come at a juncture in the history of Brook Farm when financial difficulties made the future existence of the experiment problematical. A new constitution was adopted and the society was incorporated by the state legislature. A rather complicated system of government was drawn up and the industrial organization of the community was worked out with typical Fourieristic detail—farming series, mechanical series, domestic series, and so on, each series being subdivided into many groups. For a time there appears to have been a profit-

[11] Preamble to Articles of Agreement and Association, signed by the Brook Farmers.
[12] Hinds, *op. cit.*, pp. 231–232.
[13] Frothingham's account of Brook Farm, quoted by Hinds.
[14] Hinds, *op. cit.*, p. 231.

able renewal of industrial activity, but the financial problem was still unsettled. Finally a great disaster, the destruction by fire of the large $7000 unitary building, had such a depressing effect upon the members that one by one they lost heart and departed.[15] The experiment was brought to a close in 1847 after six years of harmonious community life.

In many respects the Brook Farm experiment was a complete contrast to the New Harmony experiment. In the one, harmonious relations were enjoyed for six years by a small group of like-minded and highly cultured people who, however, failed to make their communism a financial success; in the other, friction and lack of harmony existed from the first among the heterogeneous aggregate, and although the financial backing was adequate and generous, the experiment came to a disastrous end in two years. It is difficult to draw any general conclusions from the Brook Farm experiment which will be sufficiently definite to have sociological value. The one outstanding fact, however, seems to be that like-mindedness is sometimes a more fundamental condition of community survival than material endowment. But here again, local experimentation has established no new sociological principle.

The most successful experiment in Fourieristic principles was the North American Phalanx organized August 12, 1843, near Red Bank, Monmouth County, New Jersey, and continuing with considerable prosperity for thirteen years. The New York *Tribune* described the community in 1854 as located on a domain of 673 acres of land, equipped with steam flour and saw mills, a mansion house, packing house, carpenters' shops, and blacksmiths' shops. Near the mansion house was a nursery where the children were taken care of while their mothers worked. The inhabitants numbered about 100 persons. Labor was divided into various departments occupied with fruit drying, the bottling of fruit, the cultivation of potatoes, tomatoes, turnips, melons, cucumbers, and garden seeds, the manufacture of wheat, rye, and buckwheat flour, corn meal, samp, and hominy. The labor of each person was credited by the hour and charged with board, lodging, and other things received from the

[15] *Ibid.,* pp. 233–239.

association. The balance due for excess labor value was paid in cash.

This community weathered many of the preliminary dangers which had broken up other experiments of a similar nature. There were personal difficulties and two parties contended for authority, yet neither of these factors was directly responsible for the final dissolution of the association. As late as August, 1885, a visitor to the phalanx testified to the still prevailing spirit of contentment. Yet shortly after this favorable report a difference of opinion arose concerning the location of a new mill and when the question was put to vote the majority was found to be in favor of dissolving the community.[16]

The causes of the dissolution seem to have been various. Among the chief of them was lack of educational facilities, a secession of some of the members, the burning of the mill, and dissatisfaction about the return paid for labor. It appears that there was not sufficient distinction between labor of brain and muscle. The president received only ten cents a day more than a common laborer. It is significant that wage troubles were such an important factor in causing dissatisfaction when it is recalled that the community was established for the very purpose of destroying wealth and income distinctions. Hinds makes this comment upon the fact:

"But all this talk about wage troubles, to my mind, only proves that the great objects which originally drew the members together had lost their first power over them, and that lower and more material considerations were becoming dominant in their minds and hearts." [17]

This community experiment appears to have been well endowed materially and not to have suffered much from internal dissension. What was the cause of its failure? It would seem from the foregoing enumeration of causes that the most potent factor was lack of isolation from the disturbing influences of outside society. It should be remembered that all of these community experiments [18]

[16] *Ibid.*, pp. 243, 247.

[17] *Ibid.*, p. 248.

[18] There were in all 29 Fourieristic communities in the United States with memberships of from 20 to 420 persons, with lands of from 150 to 30,000 acres, and lasting for from six months to thirteen years each. *Ibid.*, p. 224.

were carried on in a social medium, and that the guiding motives of life in surrounding society, the prejudices, the customs, the laws, the forces, and various principles of elemental human nature, were uneliminated and troublesome influences. Scientific experimentation under such limited conditions of control was impossible. It was like attempting to conduct a chemical experiment in a bowl of molasses. Consequently the conclusions from such experiments must be qualified by the unsatisfactory control of the experiment.

The condition of isolation so fundamental for successful social experimentation was never actually realized in the utopian community experiments, and it is an open question whether this prime condition can ever be enforced in social experimentation by active human interference. Sovereign states have, however, experimented upon the people without the aid of this important condition. Since the subject is obviously unlimited from the historical point of view, it will be well to confine our analysis to a few typical contemporary cases.

SOCIAL LEGISLATION IS SOCIAL EXPERIMENTATION

One of the most interesting sociological experiments of modern times, because of both its method and its scope, was the vast social insurance scheme of the German Empire. It was a case of deliberate social experimentation. It is now quite generally recognized that under the contemporary organization of industry which has resulted from the industrial revolution the great masses of working people of industrial nations receive inadequate wages as tested by the necessity of meeting the inescapable hazards of accident, sickness, death, and old age. A knowledge of this fact as well as a variety of separate contributory influences, foremost among which was several years' experience with sick benefits among labor organizations, led the German government to formulate a plan for three branches of insurance—against sickness, against industrial accident, and against old age and invalidity. These respective bills of the year 1881 became laws in 1883, in 1884, and in 1889. Under them millions of German working people were insured and received protection which they could not have secured by individual assumption of the risks.

Benefits granted under the laws were considered payments of legal obligation and not a public charity. The success of this vast experiment seems to be shown by its continuance as a settled policy during a period of great industrial and commercial expansion, and by its imitation on the part of Germany's great competitor, England. It is claimed by Germans that no small part of their country's remarkable national unity in World War I was due to the strengthening effects of 30 years of social insurance among the masses of the people.

But the German experiment was superimposed from above and does not illustrate democratic experimentation. For examples of sociological experimentation more directly initiated and sanctioned by the people we must turn to England and America. Considering the United States first, we find that social legislation on the Pacific coast constitutes a remarkable example of social experimentation.[19] The principles involved in the experimental direct legislation forms of initiative, referendum, and recall, the direct election of senators, the minimum wage and other specific labor class reforms, are too well known to require elaboration here. It will suffice to outline the scope of such legislation by quoting Professor Ogburn, who says:

The new states have not hesitated to experiment. It is well to see these experiments in summary. Oregon was the first state to adopt the recall, the direct election of senators, the presidential preference primary, to pass an extensive ten-hour law for women and to put into effect the minimum wage law for women. California was the first state in scientific budget making. Washington was first to abolish private employment bureaus and is first in the efficiency of public schools. Oregon was third to provide for the initiative and the referendum and was first to develop them. Oregon was second to adopt the direct primary and California was second to put into effect a law requiring the reporting of industrial diseases. There were only two states to precede the Pacific coast states in creating mother's pensions. In adopting other social legislation, while not the first, second or third states, Washington, Oregon and California were in a small leading group to legislate on home rule

[19] W. F. Ogburn, "Social Legislation on the Pacific Coast," *Popular Science Monthly*, March, 1915, pp. 274–289.

for cities, child labor, hours of labor on public works, factory sanitation and inspection, employers' liability, eugenics, prohibition, prison reform, public utilities, municipal ownership, the social evil and woman suffrage. The success of these experiments may be interpreted by observing the extent to which other states are following their example. . . .[20]

In the field of factory legislation some interesting effects may be observed. It has been pointed out by Professor Karl Pearson [21] that coincident with the era of factory legislation there has been a marked decline in the birth rate of women 15 to 55 years of age in the manufacturing towns. During the period 1864 to 1891, a series of factory acts was passed which applied to bleaching and dyeing works, copper, steel and iron, textile mills, and mine work restricting the labor of children by raising the age limit and cutting down the hours of work. Educational standards were raised and school attendance was enforced by the education acts of this period. As a result, the child ceased to be an economic asset to its parents till the age of 13 or 14 years. Prior to the factory acts a large family was an advantage to a workman, for the children were put to work at an early age and soon contributed to the family income. When the working-age limit was raised and the hours of labor were restricted to remedy the inhumane conditions of child labor and to provide education for the younger generation, the immediate economic value of the child was diminished. Pearson claims that the economic value of the child of the laboring classes will in the long run govern its production. Hence the decline in the birth rate of the English laboring classes. But he also claims that the decrease in quantity has not been compensated by better quality, as is ordinarily held, for he maintains that the first-born members of a family are more likely to be abnormal, i.e., neurotic, insane, tuberculous, and albinotic, than those subsequently born.[22] Whether we accept the last corollary or not,[23] the diminished birth rate is an

[20] *Ibid.*, p. 289.

[21] *The Problem of Practical Eugenics.*

[22] *Ibid.*, pp. 19–21.

[23] K. Pearson, *On the Handicapping of the First-Born*, 1914, and criticism of Pearson's memoir by L. I. Dublin and H. Langman in *Quarterly Publication of the American Statistical Association*, December, 1915.

undoubted fact and an unexpected sequel to the factory acts, which shows that all conditions in the experiment were not known at its beginning.

The Difficulties of Experimentation in Sociology

The foregoing account supplements the general impression that the results of much experimental social legislation are as yet indefinite and inconclusive. The difficulty seems to be that every problem is more complex than was first suspected, and in the present state of our knowledge some unforeseen factor usually appears to upset our plans and invalidate our conclusions. In other words, few of the conditions of the experiment are known and consequently it is not possible to attain control. Is this fact fatal for the experimental method in sociology?

We have seen that the method of experiment was to vary one condition at a time and keep others constant or under control. But how are we to know what the others are? Only by the method of trial and error are the other conditions discovered. In the early development of the now exact physical sciences, trial and error was the only method which led to discovery. By this rough method the main conditions have been discovered and the way has been blocked out. At the present time, with many conditions known, there is a considerable field of experimentation in physical science that is mere repetition by control of conditions previously discovered. The physicist may now set up an experiment with great precision and attain definite results. It may, therefore, be legitimate to distinguish two stages in the experimental method—a pioneer stage of empirical experimentation by the rough trial-and-error method, and a precise stage when many conditions are known and controlled.

If this distinction is approximately true, then the record of social experimentation would seem to show that the sociologist is still in the first stage of the experimental method. Will he ever attain the second or precise stage?

Let us first analyze the meaning of the statement that sociological experimentation is in the pioneer, trial-and-error stage.

The method of trial and error is a law of very general application in the realm of living things. Regarded from a philosophical point of view natural selection might be said to be simply the operation of the method of trial and error in the physical world. Organic life is continuously putting out tentatives in the form of spontaneous variations. Some of these variations persist, others perish. Natural selection is the term used to describe the process by which some variations are selected and others rejected. The agents of natural selection are: limitation of food and water supply, drought, climatic change, extremes of heat and cold, storms, wild animals, genetic increase, etc. These agents act upon the structures of organic individuals, producing immediate effects in the extermination of most individuals with inadapted structures and ultimate results in the survival and perpetuation of individuals with adapted structures. It appears that organic individuals are significant and important from the evolutionary point of view only as they bear and transmit adapted structures. By this trial-and-error method nature finally evolves her adapted type of inhabiting species.

In society there is an analogous process in the principle of social selection. Human beings are continuously putting out tentatives in the form of individual and collective reactions to stimuli. Repetition of these reactions produces habit in the individual and custom in the group. Individual variations from the conduct approved by the group constitute the raw material of social selection. Innovators and radicals are subjected to group pressure to change their ways and to conform. Thus the agents of social selection—group ostracism, persecution, and punishment—act upon individuals with anti-social ways, and produce immediate effects in the extermination of anti-social individuals or in the repression of anti-social ways. The ultimate results are seen in the survival and perpetuation of adapted ways and customs. Thus human individuals attain significance from the social evolutionary point of view only as they bear and transmit adapted habits and customs.

But unlike natural selection, social selection attains its results, the survival and perpetuation of adaptations, by two processes. It is necessary to distinguish these two levels in social selection in order to apprehend the true significance of the trial-and-error method in

society. Natural selection secures the essential adaptation by extermination of inadapted forms. Social selection accomplishes adaptation (in habit and custom) in primitive stages of social development, and to a lessening degree in higher stages, by the extermination of anti-social individuals; but adaptation is also secured by
social control which falls short of life destruction and simply re-
presses and constrains.

It is this second aspect of social selection which marks it off from
natural selection as a more discriminating process. The survival of
adapted structures cannot be attained by any means other than the
extermination of individuals with inadapted structures, since the
structure cannot be separated from the individual and because the
laws of physical heredity are rigid. If the non-transmissibility of
acquired characteristics were not so generally substantiated as a
principle of evolution, we might look for the perpetuation of adaptations without physical extermination. On the other hand, the
significant thing for society is habit and custom, traits which can be
separated from the individual and modified in the individual. Hence
adaptation in habit and custom may be secured by constraint.
Ostracism, persecution, and punishment are some of the forms of
social pressure which lead individuals with anti-social habits and
customs to rearrange their mode of conduct and conform to the
approved standards. Much of modern educational practice is based
upon this fundamental principle.

If it is permissible, as it seems to the author, to roughly distinguish
two methods in social selection, it would be well to differentiate
between them in terminology. The author, therefore, uses the term
"social selection" to designate the process by which society secures
adaptation in individual habit and conduct through the means of
excluding or exterminating anti-social individuals, and the term
"societal selection" to designate the process by which society secures
the preservation of adapted habits and customs by means of social
constraint.

This distinction is in no sense identical with that made by Professor Albert G. Keller [24] between automatic and rational selection as

[24] *Societal Evolution*, 1915, especially chaps. 3, 4, and 5.

forms of the general social process which he calls societal selection. The author considers that Keller's distinction is not more fundamental than this one. Moreover, the distinction just made enables the sociologist to avoid the looser sort of analogical reasoning and to see at once into the heart of the selective process of society. For example, social selection, as defined above, may be both automatic and rational: the group may react suddenly and under stress of emotion cast out or kill the offender, as in the case of a lynching; or the group may exclude or kill the offender after mature deliberation, as in criminal procedure. Similarly, societal selection, as defined above, may be both automatic and rational: the group may react quite thoughtlessly and require conformity to the established customs, as in the ostracism of Gorki; or the group may consider the situation carefully and decide to abolish the offending custom or way, as when a legislature repeals a statute and enacts a new law to take its place with due provision for enforcement and penalties. (The passage of a law which punishes felony with imprisonment or death is an example of rational societal selection, whereas the operation of the law, by which the felon is separated from society and imprisoned, is an example of rational social selection.)

It should now be clear that collective experimentation of the sort to be compared with the experimental method of the physical scientist is simply rational societal selection.[25] But rational selection, as illustrated by the procedure of legislative enactment, the initiative, the referendum, and by the decisions of semi-public or class legislative bodies, is simply the trial-and-error method carried on by collective action.

The truth of this statement will be recognized when one considers the vast amount of legislation which fails to correct the evils it aims at, and when one considers the numerous group and class experiments that have been inconclusive or even disastrous failures. We are now beginning to understand that legislation and all social experimentation should be guided by a more accurate knowledge of facts. Lester F. Ward said:

[25] *Ibid.*, chaps. 4, 5.

When the people become so intelligent that they know how to choose as their representatives, persons of decided ability, who know something of human nature, who recognize that there are social forces, and that their duty is to devise ways and means for scientifically controlling those forces on exactly the same principles that an experimenter or an inventor controls the forces of physical nature, then we may look for scientific legislation.[26]

Again,

It must not be supposed that such legislation can be conducted to any considerable extent in the open sessions of legislative bodies. These will doubtless need to be maintained, and every new law should be finally adopted by a vote of such bodies, but more and more this will become merely a formal way of putting the final sanction of society on decisions that have been carefully worked out in what may be called the sociological laboratory. Legislation will consist in a series of exhaustive experiments on the part of true scientific sociologists and sociological inventors working on the problems of social physics from the practical point of view. It will undertake to solve not only questions of general interest to the state—the maintenance of revenues without compulsion and without friction and a smooth and peaceful conduct of all the operations of a nation—but questions of social improvement, and amelioration of the condition of all the people, the removal of whatever privation may still remain, and the adoption of means to the positive increase of the social welfare, in short the organization of human happiness.[27]

We are still in the trial-and-error stage of overt social experimentation. It will be some time before all the conditions of any social problem are known and probably many years before precise experimentation is possible. But assuming that the sociologist will eventually attain a state of more complete knowledge of social conditions such that the factors entering into any social problem are known, may he not then pass into the precise stage of overt social experimentation?

The difficulty which prevents precise methods in sociological experimentation is inherent in its data. Social units are complex as

[26] *Applied Sociology*, 1906, p. 338.
[27] *Ibid.*, also *Dynamic Sociology*, vol. ii, p. 156.

compared with the relatively simple units of other sciences. In physical science the units operated upon are homogeneous, standardized; whether in China or in America, given the controlled conditions, the experiment will work; it may be repeated. But in sociology the units are not homogeneous or standardized; every unit is unique, individual, different; moreover, there is the constant bias of race, government, standard of living, and political ideals. An experiment in China proves little or nothing for America. Welfare experiments, housing reforms, model villages, unemployment insurance, though successful in Germany and England, prove nothing final and conclusive for Americans. Every one of these schemes must be rearranged and adapted to American conditions before it will work—and then the result may be something new, quite unlike the European model. Moreover, while the sociologist is experimenting with human units the factors change, the problem assumes a new aspect, as when legislation to correct an abuse comes after some unforeseen economic factor has already eliminated the evil. Thus do fundamental differences in race, government, political ideals, and standard of living constitute the uncontrolled conditions which invalidate conclusions that may be drawn from much social experimentation.

TRIAL AND ERROR, PLANNING AND PREDICTION

Trial-and-error responses to a novel social situation may take the form of planning. It may be helpful to distinguish between the somewhat blind process of trial and error on the one hand, and of planning and prediction on the other hand.[28] To do this we may first inquire: What does the concept "trial and error" stand for? What does the concept "planning" stand for? What does the concept "prediction" stand for? One answer to these questions may be found in a simple application of semantics.[29]

[28] The following portions of this chapter appeared originally in an article, "The Relation of Sociometry to Planning in an Expanding Social Universe," by F. Stuart Chapin, in *Sociometry*, August, 1943, pp. 234–240.

[29] For a more technical discussion of this method, see the author's article, "The Syntactical Analysis of Sociometric Techniques: Cases in Point," *Sociometry*, May, 1941, pp. 177–183. Also chap. VI, pp. 157–164.

Table 1 presents a schematic analysis of several interrelated concepts which are widely used in discussions of post-war problems. The first row in the first column carries the entry, "Trial and error on overt level," because this is the beginning of all exploratory behavior that seeks the solution of some problem which a human being faces. When we say that so-and-so is attempting to solve his problem by trial and error what do we mean? What does the concept or phrase stand for? What are its referents? In the second column of row 1 we make the entry, "Manipulation of objects into different arrangements." This is the referent of the term; it is what it stands for; it is its meaning. We may now put the two together and assert, "Trial and error on the overt level is the manipulation of objects into different arrangements." Thus we see that the concept, trial and error, has fact referents, observed differences in kind or perhaps in degree.

All concepts and terms do not, however, have such easily observed fact referents. Indeed, some terms widely used in problem-solving behavior seem to have no fact referents composed of sense perceptions. This would seem to be the case with such terms as "intuition" or "hunch." What is the referent of this term? To answer this question we are obliged to resort to other terms or words. We say that the hunch is merely guessing. Thus some concepts seem to have only linguistic referents.

This was the situation for a long time with respect to the term "atom." Now, however, physical research using refined measurements has advanced to the stage to which our senses respond to fluctuations in delicately balanced physical instruments which in turn reflect differences in atomic structures too minute to be recorded directly by our rather crude human sensory apparatus. The process of scientific measurement, in short, extends our powers of sense perception by interposing delicate physical instruments between our sense perceptors and minute differences in physical substances. This process of scientific advance is also seen in cruder form in the use of carefully calibrated attitude scales which enable us to note small differences in the strength of beliefs about social issues, differences too slight to be noted in ordinary conversation. Since sociometry

TABLE 1. Concepts and Their Referents

Concepts and Terms	Referents			
	Having Fact Referents Observed as Differences in		Having Linguistic (or Numerical) Referents	
	Kind	Degree	Potential Fact Referents	Purely Linguistic
(1)	(2)	(3)	(4)	(5)
1. Trial and error on overt level	Manipulation of objects into different arrangements			
2. Trial and error on covert or thought level			Manipulation of terms or words that stand for sense experience. Empirical predictions [a] and empirical planning [b] ↓ ↓	← Concepts or terms stand for imagined objects or arrangement of objects
3. Prediction (scientific)			Extrapolation from measured trend lines, concepts based on measurements	← Concepts or terms acquire potential fact referents
4. Planning (scientific)			Master plans; engineering blueprints; inventor's models. Concepts based on experiments	← Concepts or terms acquire potential fact referents
5. Intuition (scientific)			↑ (?) ← Terms stand for memories or images of past experiences, not organized at the focus of critical attention or observation, but general and non-specific	— Mere guessing, because concepts or terms have only class names or group names as referents, no specific objects or specific arrangements

[a] Prediction is a preparatory reaction seeking adjustment now to an anticipated (feared or desired) future need or event or consequence which is represented by words or visual images. It is a reaction to a substitute stimulus of symbols.

[b] Planning is essentially trial and error on the thought level to avoid wasteful trial and error on the overt level. It is a form of substitute response in which words or visual images that stand for real things are manipulated in advance of the physical manipulations of the real things for which the symbols stand.

defined as social measurement includes the construction and calibration of scales to measure social attitudes, it at once becomes evident that sociometry has the power to extend sensory perceptions to the realm of formerly imperceptible variations in belief about social issues. In this way, the term "guessing," which is originally a mere linguistic referent for the concept "intuition," may perhaps be given specificity and in time come to attain the more objective condition of having at least potential fact referents—see row 5, column (4). We shall presently return to the problem of intuition, but it may be said parenthetically that we have completed and published one paper which demonstrated the possibility of giving a concept such as "social insight," ordinarily regarded as an intangible, a potential fact referent in a sociometric scale, a scale which differentiates significantly by scores between the clerical workers and the executives of the same organization.[30]

If this explanation of the processes by which a concept that originally had only linguistic referents comes to attain the stage of having at least potential fact referents is clear to the reader, we are now ready to tackle the semantic analysis of other concepts, such as trial and error on the thought level, prediction, and planning.

Since the first approach to prediction and planning is a process that may be called trial and error on the covert or thought level, let us inquire into the referents of this concept. What is it that we do when we think? We manipulate words or images that usually stand for objects (as in reverie). Unlike overt trial and error where the real objects are put in successive arrangements, we manipulate words and memory images when we think. In trial and error on the thought level we therefore manipulate the words or memory images (symbols) that stand for objects that presumably have or had existence, e.g., words or images that stand for sensory experience. This is the crude empirical level of planning and prediction.

In scientific prediction and planning we also manipulate concepts, terms, words, and memory images, but these have at least potential fact referents. Now it is in the weakness of the correspondence be-

---

[30] "Preliminary Standardization of a Social Insight Scale," *American Sociological Review*, April, 1942, pp. 214–225.

tween these terms or images (symbols) and the real things they represent (other factors being held constant) that we find the limitations of scientific planning and prediction. Two methods have been developed in science to provide this exact correspondence: one is by scientific measurements [31] and the other by the method of experiment.

Social experimentation by overt trial and error seeks to achieve some *desired change* in social relations. As such, it may be distinguished from experimental designs which seek to *obtain observations* of social relations under conditions of control. The latter is the subject of this book. If experimental designs facilitate the discovery of cause-and-effect relationships in society, then the knowledge thus obtained may be used to direct the course of social change, and substitute for a blind trial-and-error process a more rational guidance of social relations.

In these methods of experimental design and measurement, numerical expressions stand for differences in degree of different kinds of experience. Numerical expressions so used have the advantage of easy manipulation and, more important still, they are susceptible of verification. Thus we make measurements, plot trend lines, and extrapolate observations within the limits of probability; or we conduct controlled experiments and from these make master plans, engineering blueprints, or inventor's models.

From this analysis the importance of measurement is readily seen. Measurement is at the very center of all scientific advances. Social measurement, or sociometry, is still in its beginnings. Yet there seems no good reason to think that it may not in time become much more precise than it is at present, even though it may never attain the accuracy of physical measurements.

Another glance at our table suggests certain logical interrelationships that are of use in understanding the possibilities of sociometry. In the first place, trial and error on the thought level in its empirical stage opens up the possibility of prediction and planning in a scientific stage. In the second place, scientific prediction and planning in limited areas and with near-by objectives leads to less wasteful

[31] *Ibid.*

trial and error on the overt level with larger units and more distant objectives. Sociometry, by promoting measurement and experimentation, may contribute to the exactness of the correspondence between social concepts and the social referents for which the concepts stand. This should facilitate social planning and social prediction with respect to limited objectives. Any improvement in planning for or prediction of limited objectives facilitates trial and error that involves larger units and more distant objectives because it reduces the waste of trial and error on large-scale problems approached blindly.

Finally let us return to the concept of intuition. The disrepute into which this term has fallen among many scientists is due to the fact that it is used without proper discrimination; for instance, if intuition is to be regarded as a tool of research to be set alongside measurement and experiment, only confusion results. Intuition does not describe objects of sensory experience. It is not a form of scientific description. If it is used in this sense, it becomes an escape-from-reality device which helps wishful thinkers find what they desire to find. This is the use of the term that is properly condemned because it leads over imperceptibly into clairvoyance, telepathy, premonitions, mystic insight, and similar delusions. But on the other hand, if intuition is regarded as a process of thinking in which the purpose is explanation of dim memory, it may yield useful results. We would, therefore, define intuition as a process. The intuitive process consists of a convergence of as yet unverbalized experience (because only organically recorded) into a pattern of response below the threshold of critical attention; this pattern may then emerge in part and, when verbalized, serves as a partial explanation of the problem which acted as the original stimulus. Intuition is then a judgment based on the convergence and integration of former impressions of memory into a pattern of explanation in which the perceptual details are not at the threshold of critical attention.

This definition has the merit of using as referents terms that stand for memories or images of past experience and thus takes the concept out of the purely linguistic type of referents and transfers it into an area of potential fact referents. Since it is known that intuitions sometimes lead to valid explanations and offer clues to eventual solution of problems (both practical and scientific), it would appear that this definition is serviceable. We may understand how the intuitive process, so defined, may lead to fruitful working hypotheses which stimulate planning and prediction in the meaning defined in rows 4 and 5 and columns 4 and 5 of our table.

We may therefore conclude that the concepts, trial and error on the overt level, trial and error on the thought level, prediction, planning, and intuition are all interrelated in the process of social research, and that a sociometry which provides measurements to make more exact the correspondence between these concepts and the things for which they stand may make a useful contribution to our understanding and control of human behavior in an expanding social universe.

Chapter II

THREE EXPERIMENTAL DESIGNS FOR CONTROLLED OBSERVATION

THE concept of experimental design in sociological research refers to systematic study of human relations by making observations under conditions of control.

Control of social conditions is obtained not by manipulating people or by exerting any physical force on persons. The control is obtained by *selecting* for observation two groups of like individuals, for example, individuals of the same income bracket, the same occupational class, the same chronological age, the same size of family, the same intelligence quotient, etc. (by matching on these attributes). Then one group, called the experimental group, is given treatment, or receives some social program, or is subjected to some assumed and uncontrolled natural force (F) in the environment, while the other group, called the control group, is denied this treatment, program, or force (F). Observations or measurements on a sociometric scale are then made on each group at some beginning date (before) and again at the termination of a period of months or years (after). Finally, comparative changes in the mean measurements at each date are noted. If the change in the experimental group is of a magnitude that could occur very infrequently as a fluctuation of random sampling, whereas the change in the control group is of a magnitude that may occur frequently as a fluctuation of random sampling, we conclude that the change in the experimental group is *probably* an effect of the treatment, social program, or assumed natural force (F) in the environment. In this way experimental design is a form of controlled observation operating by the agency of selective control of conditions which for purposes of observation it is desirable to hold constant. But no proof can be accepted short of confirmation of the results by repeating the study under like conditions.

Experimental design does not mean attempts to improve human relations by controls designed to guide change toward some desired end. These efforts at reform may be made the *subject matter* of experimental design studies, as will be seen in the following accounts of studies that attempt to test by changes in measurements the effects of reform programs of public housing, rural hygiene, work relief, counseling of university students, and treatment of juvenile delinquents. Confusion in thought only results when there is failure to distinguish between the means-ends schema of social reform programs, on the one hand, and on the other hand the use of experimental designs to *study* assumed cause-and-effect relationships. In social reform a desired end is set and various means are tried to achieve this end. In experimental design studies the student is an observer and not an active agent of social reform or change. Does improved housing (as a means chosen by the social reformer) achieve better personal adjustment and improved morale (the ends-in-view)? An answer to this question is sought in studies by experimental design to discover if improved housing (as an assumed cause) is followed invariably by better personal adjustment and improved morale (as an effect). But since personal adjustment and morale are influenced by many other factors than housing, that is, by income, employment, occupation, size of family, years of formal education, etc., it becomes necessary to control these factors if we are to observe changes in measured adjustment and in morale, which we assume to be associated with change in housing from crowded slum dwellings to more adequate modern dwellings of a public housing project. Despite the fact that studies by experimental design have not yet succeeded in clearly isolating the complex housing factor per se, it may be contended that such studies do point the way that can lead to more complete knowledge of social cause-and-effect relationships.

Studies by experimental design may be applied also in an attempt to discover assumed cause-and-effect relationships that operate in society quite apart from changes made by programs of social reform. Thus the study of tuberculosis death rates in New York City [1] shows

[1] See chap. v, pp. 124–139.

that significant declines in the tuberculosis death rate from 1930 to 1940 occur in health areas that had high rentals in 1930, and that no significant decline in tuberculosis death rate occurred in health areas that had low rentals in 1930. To be sure, this does not *prove* that high rentals as an economic force were a cause per se of lowered tuberculosis death rates, but it does *suggest* the importance of prior economic status as a bundle of factors representing social forces in the community which cause change in the tuberculosis death rate, and thus adds confirmation to a hypothesis of economic causation.

If studies using experimental design do not prove the existence of specific cause-and-effect relationships, of what use are such studies? In the first place, it may be noted that the qualification "do not prove" is introduced because these are single studies and have not been repeated. It is a condition of all scientific experimentation that repetition under like conditions with like results, or verification, is insisted upon as the criterion of proof. Although there are real obstacles to repetition [2] of such experimental design studies, these are not insuperable. In the second place, many unknown factors remain uncontrolled in the present stage of development of experimental designs. But, given time for improvement in techniques of research, there is no reason to believe that our ability to identify and control additional factors will not grow. And in the third place, the experimental designs herein discussed are to be regarded in their present crude stage of development as purely exploratory and as leading to tentative conclusions which, although they may serve as pre-tests of working hypotheses for further research, are still always subject to verification by replication.

Research in the biological sciences [3] and in educational psychology [4] utilizes numerous designs for experiment. In sociological research three broad designs only have been selected for elaboration in this book. In the study of social relations we are interested in the present,

[2] See chap. VII, pp. 187–189.

[3] R. A. Fisher, *The Design of Experiments,* Oliver & Boyd, 1942.

[4] E. F. Lindquist, *Statistical Analysis in Educational Research,* Houghton Mifflin, 1940, pp. 80–84.

in the future, and in the past. The three experimental designs chosen for analysis in the chapters that follow illustrate applications to existing problems (the present), to problems of "before" and "after" (the future), and to a method of tracing from a present problem back in time to a prior assumed cause (the past). These designs may be briefly defined as follows (see Table 2):

TABLE 2.   Comparison of Types of Experimental Design

TYPE OF DESIGN (1)	THE PAST "Before" (2)	THE PRESENT (3)	THE FUTURE "After" (4)
1. Cross-sectional design	0	Exp. group 1 2 3[a] Control group	0
2. Projected design	0	Exp. group 1 2 3 Control group	Exp group ? 1 2 3 Control group ?
3. Ex post facto design	? Exp. group 1 2 3 ? Control group	Exp. group 1 2 3 Control group	0

[a] The numbers 1, 2, and 3, between the experimental group and the control group refer to factors controlled by matching, an operation that will be described in detail in the chapters that follow.

1. *Cross-sectional design,* which makes controlled comparisons for a single date by procedures of selective control. Studies of this sort appear in Chapter III.

2. *A projected design* of "before" and "after" study, in which an attempt is made to measure the effects of a social program or social force at some future date, thus following through the flow of events from a present date to some future date, by procedures of selective control. Studies of this sort appear in Chapter IV.

3. *An ex post facto design,* in which some present effect is traced backward to an assumed causal complex of factors or forces at a prior date, using for this purpose such records as are available, since no new measures of the past can be made in the present, and relying as before on procedures of selective control. Studies of this sort appear in Chapter V.

Chapter III

CROSS–SECTIONAL EXPERIMENTAL
DESIGN

ARE SOCIAL programs, or the treatment given one group of persons, more closely associated with acceptable personal adjustment than is found to be the case among a group of persons without such programs or treatment? A preliminary answer to this question, based upon the facts of a single date, may suggest the desirability of more extensive study over intervals of time. Cross-sectional experimental design is a method of study of this problem which, if it reveals a relationship encouraging research of a more ambitious sort, serves the useful function of an exploratory effort.

The task of measuring relationships is performed by statistical methods when correlation coefficients are computed. But since the measure of association between two factors, with numerous other factors unknown, does not lead to reliable knowledge, we need to introduce control over these other factors in our observational procedures. This may be done by partial correlation analysis, which is a powerful tool for measuring the relationship between two factors while one or more other measured factors are held constant. It is, however, not advisable to use partial correlation unless certain conditions of reliable initial measurements, homogeneity, sampling, and normality of distribution are met. Hence resort is often made to some breakdown analysis [1] in which homogeneous sub-groups are sorted out and simple correlations then made within these sub-groups. When such an analysis yields high correlations we appear to have discovered a persistent or real relationship, which was obscured in the larger and more heterogeneous group.

Analysis by cross-sectional experimental design *makes homogeneous* the two groups to be compared—the experimental group

[1] Manual manipulation.

which receives the program or treatment and the control group which is denied this program or treatment—and does so by matching the measurements on selected factors. Sometimes this control is achieved by identical individual matching; but more often it is approximated by equating frequency distributions on a given trait. In either case, some degree of control of *known* factors is obtained so that any increase in the measured relationship of the two factors, treatment and adjustment, which results increases our knowledge of association but does not establish the existence of a cause-and-effect relationship. It may, however, provide additional evidence in support of a working hypothesis and thus encourage us to undertake the projected experimental design described in Chapter IV, as a procedure to discover if a cause-and-effect relationship exists. In any event, analysis of association by cross-sectional experimental design forces us to handle the data, and the matching process adds to our store of direct knowledge of the factors in the problem. This point has been argued with good effect by Ezekiel[2] and deserves more attention than it has received from research sociologists.

Two examples of cross-sectional analysis by experimental design may now be considered: the personal adjustment of Boy Scouts in Minneapolis in 1938 and the personal adjustment of work relief clients compared with direct relief clients in St. Paul in 1939.

THE PERSONAL ADJUSTMENT OF BOY SCOUTS[3]

Mandel[4] set out to analyze the relationship between the duration of Boy Scout tenure in the Minneapolis area and subsequent participation in community activities and in community adjustments of these Boy Scouts four years after leaving the organization. Large sums are spent annually in the belief that the program

[2] M. Ezekiel, *Methods of Correlation Analysis.* Wiley, 2nd ed., 1941; see also, for partial correlation, Margaret J. Hagood, *Statistics for Sociologists,* Reynal & Hitchcock, 1941, pp. 717–746, and G. U. Yule and M. G. Kendall, *An Introduction to the Theory of Statistics,* Griffin, 1940, pp. 261–287.

[3] This section of the chapter was formerly published as part of an article, "Design for Social Experiments," in the *American Sociological Review,* December, 1938, pp. 796–800.

[4] "A Controlled Analysis of the Relationship of Boy Scout Tenure and Participation to Community Adjustment," M.A. thesis, University of Minnesota, July, 1938.

of the Boy Scouts of America "builds character." The national officials directing the program are aware of this problem and have encouraged a number of studies to evaluate the results of the program.[5] The Mandel study differs from all other studies previously made in that it is a more thoroughgoing application of the experimental method. Its results are consistent with earlier results in so far as comparability is possible. No attempt was made in the Mandel study to test the building of character. As we shall see, a simpler and more limited objective was studied.

The procedure was as follows: From the 2050 cards in the 1934 drop-file of the Metropolitan Division of the Minneapolis Area Council, a random sample of every tenth case was taken. This gave 205 individuals. Next, an effort was made to follow up all of these former Scouts. A total of 102 were located and personally interviewed in 1938. The remaining 103 could not be located, had moved away, were deceased, or were not cooperative. The sample of 102 was then divided into groups. The first group had dropped out of scouting during the year 1934 with an average tenure of 1.3 years. This was called the control group of drop-out Scouts. The second group consisted of Scouts who had completed an average of 4 years of tenure by the year 1934. This was called the experimental group of active Scouts. Next, the two groups were paired by equating the frequency distributions on place of birth (rural or urban), father's occupation, health rating on the Bell test, and age-grade ratio (a rough rating on mental ability). Enforcing these four controls eliminated 22 individuals, so that the final control group of drop-out Scouts consisted of 40 boys, and the experimental group of active Scouts consisted also of 40 boys. In the course of the interview in 1938, each of these 80 Scouts was scored for participation on the Social Participation Scale,[6] a scoring device developed by Chapin in 1927 and since then partially standardized for reliability and validity, on the Bell Adjustment Inventory,[7] and on the Rundquist-

---

[5] *Ibid.*, pp. 28–49, 86–89.

[6] F. Stuart Chapin, *Social Participation Scale,* University of Minnesota Press, 1937. (See Appendix B.)

[7] High M. Bell, *The Adjustment Inventory,* Stanford University Press, 1934.

Sletto[8] scales of morale and general adjustment. These latter are all fully standardized scales with established reliabilities and validities. Thus the Mandel experiment, although it used the crude control technique of equated frequency distributions rather than identical individual pairing, used as measures of adjustment scales that had been previously standardized and widely used.

The results of this experiment showed that the active Scouts of 1934 had a better adjustment in 1938 than the drop-out Scouts did on both the Bell and the Rundquist-Sletto adjustment scales. This characteristic is supplemented by a record of fewer delinquencies and delinquencies of less serious nature on the part of active Scouts than of drop-out Scouts. Thus, the slight measured differences in adjustment (not statistically significant) are supported and reinforced by the evidence of non-quantified factors and demonstrate the value of the criterion of agreement among small differences.

There was, however, one marked difference of statistical significance, and that was the participation score of 11.00 points, the average for the 40 drop-out Scouts, and the participation score of 5.82 points, the average for the active Scouts. Here we find a difference of 5.18 between the two group means, or a drop-out group score which is 89 per cent higher than the active group score in 1938. Mandel points out that this difference, which is statistically significant, may be due to the desire of individual boys in the drop-out group not to "channelize" their participation into scouting alone, but to diversify their participation in other activities. Active Scouts seem to concentrate all of their interests in one activity. The higher social participation score of the drop-out Scouts may be explained as due to: (1) their search for a basis of integration for their individual desires, since the active Scouts may have found already *within* the varied program of the Scout organization a framework of integration not easily possible from participation in diverse community groups; or (2) their wish not *to narrow down* their activities to one type of organization at such an early age, motivated by the *wish* for new experience and

[8] E. A. Rundquist and R. F. Sletto, *Minnesota Survey of Opinions* (short form), 1936, pp. 394–398 in *Personality in the Depression,* University of Minnesota Press, 1936.

the *wish* for response, which they satisfied in taking part in a variety of activities; or (3) their *greater intensity* (more memberships on committees and more official positions held) as well as *greater extensity* (memberships in a larger number of organizations); or (4) the fact that they were more *socially acceptable* than active Scouts to admission into a large variety of community activities. Since the drop-outs were a more variable group and more non-conformist in behavior, it seems probable that explanations (1), (2), and (3) are true, rather than (4). The fact that the drop-outs were slightly less well adjusted on the Bell and Rundquist-Sletto scale norms tends also to minimize the value of explanation (4). In general, all the evidence of this experiment tends to show that boys who had stayed four years in scouting and thus secured the full benefit of the scout program up to the year 1934 were on the whole a more conventional, conforming, and homogeneous group in 1938 than the drop-out group. The latter was more variable, less conventional, and more non-conformist in 1938.

If it be accepted that the valid measure of adjustment is based upon attitudinal factors expressed in verbal responses measured by the Bell and Rundquist-Sletto scales, then the criterion of agreement among small differences is in favor of the active Scouts. On the other hand, if it be held that evidence of overt participation in community activities is a better measure of community adjustment, then the strikingly higher score of the drop-out Scouts indicates that they are the better adjusted. The final conclusion is then a matter of judgment. Evidently it is necessary to do additional research on this problem. It would be advantageous to repeat the experiment using similar techniques under like conditions.

Our design for social experiments may be summarized in visual form. We present this summary in Figures 1 and 2 using some of the data of the Mandel experiment to make the exhibit definitive. Figure 1 shows the general procedure followed in the use of the experimental method and indicates graphically the successive steps and the corresponding shrinkage in the size of sample observed. Figure 2 shows the more detailed technical aspects of using the technique of control by equating the frequency distributions of four variables which it is desired to hold constant. It also shows the relationship between the measured free variables. Thus, longer Scout tenure (an average of 4 years for the experimental group) is associated with a significantly lower score on social participation,

FIGURE 1. Design for Social Experiments [a]

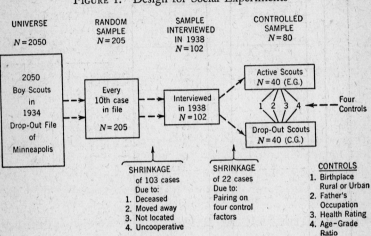

UNIVERSE
$N = 2050$

RANDOM SAMPLE
$N = 205$

SAMPLE INTERVIEWED IN 1938
$N = 102$

CONTROLLED SAMPLE
$N = 80$

2050 Boy Scouts in 1934 Drop-Out File of Minneapolis

Every 10th case in file
$N = 205$

Interviewed in 1938
$N = 102$

Active Scouts
$N = 40$ (E.G.)

1 2 3 4 ← Four Controls

Drop-Out Scouts
$N = 40$ (C.G.)

SHRINKAGE of 103 cases Due to:
1. Deceased
2. Moved away
3. Not located
4. Uncooperative

SHRINKAGE of 22 cases Due to: Pairing on four control factors

CONTROLS
1. Birthplace Rural or Urban
2. Father's Occupation
3. Health Rating
4. Age-Grade Ratio

[a] Based on Mandel data.

and shorter Scout tenure (an average of 1.3 years for the control group of drop-outs) is associated with a social participation score that is 89 per cent higher. The slight differences in the adjustment scores are not shown on the chart because of the difficulty of representing four-dimensional variation on a flat surface. Nevertheless, the charts serve to present the main outlines of a design for social experiment. It may be remarked parenthetically that this design for experiment is substantially the same as the schematic pattern we presented in 1931 and subsequently published in *Social Forces*.[9]

[9] F. Stuart Chapin, "The Advantages of Experimental Sociology in the Study of Family Group Patterns," *Social Forces*, December, 1932.

FIGURE 2. Design for Social Experiments [a]

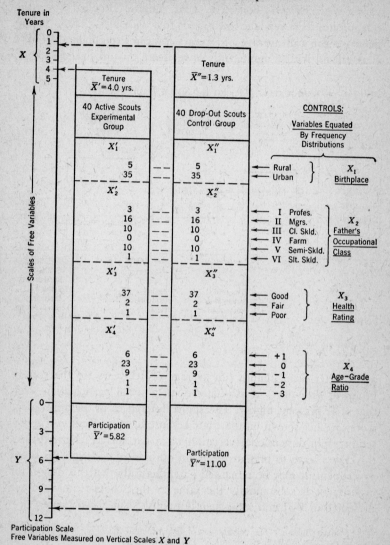

Participation Scale
Free Variables Measured on Vertical Scales X and Y

[a] Based on Mandel data.

The Personal Adjustment of Work Relief Clients [10]

A program of work projects for the able-bodied, needy unemployed is generally assumed to have two important advantages over a system of direct relief. In the first place, it is obvious that such a program results in additions to the facilities and services of a community—public buildings, roads, educational activities, etc.—which would not be possible otherwise. The second advantage involves the maintenance and development of skills, work habits, and morale among the unemployed.

Despite the fact that the value of a work relief program in maintaining the morale of the unemployed is widely accepted, objective evidence on the question is fragmentary. This study attempts to provide an answer to the question, Does work relief maintain a higher morale than direct relief? Since an investigation of this nature concerns a study of psychological factors, and since these factors must be spontaneously expressed if they are to reveal actual differences in morale, this investigation was carried on quietly and without publicity.

The morale of eighty WPA workers in St. Paul was found to be 5.46 per cent higher than the morale of a matched group of 42 direct-relief clients in St. Paul (certified for WPA and waiting assignment). Besides measurement of morale, we obtained a pattern of adjustment by using three additional criteria—general adjustment, social participation, and social status. The average percentage superiority of the WPA workers over the matched group of direct-relief clients was 5.67 per cent on the percentage gains of these four criteria. Assuming these four criteria of adjustment to be a pattern that is more reliable than any one of the factors considered alone, we may ask: Is the difference in pattern of adjustment one that may occur so often by chance that it is merely a sampling error and not significant?

[10] This portion of the chapter was originally published in an article by the author and J. A. Jahn, "The Advantages of Work Relief over Direct Relief in Maintaining Morale in St. Paul in 1939," in the *American Journal of Sociology*, July, 1940, pp. 13–22. The Division of Research of the Work Projects Administration, which cooperated in making records available and in supplying information on administrative procedures, has given us permission to release the results of this study.

We cannot, of course, claim that the superiority of the WPA workers studied was exclusively the effect of the WPA program as a cause. But we can answer the question: What is the probability of obtaining

TABLE 3.   Differences on Four Criteria of Adjustment
WPA and Direct-Relief Groups

Groups Compared	Mean Scores on Four Criteria of Adjustment			
	Morale [a]	General Adjustment [a]	Social Participation	Social Status
WPA group, 80 cases.........	64.01	48.41	4.94	66.29
Direct-relief group, 42 cases....	67.71	50.98	4.67	62.29
Differences between mean scores.................	− 3.70	− 2.57	0.27	4.00
Percentage differences.......	5.46	5.04	5.78	6.42
Critical ratios of these differences [b]................	− 1.92	− 1.73	0.20	0.81
Combined critical ratios of four differences [c].......	....	2.33	Odds against chance occurrence, 49:1	

[a] Scores on morale and general adjustment are on reverse scales, i.e., the higher the score the worse the morale, hence a negative difference is a gain. On the last two scales an increase in score is a gain.

[b] Computed from Fisher's formula.

[c] Computed from Guttman's formula, "On Uses of the Critical Ratio," by Louis Guttman, a research paper for the M.A. degree, University of Minnesota, June, 1939, pp. 36–40. Guttman proves that although the means of two variables are correlated in random samples, nevertheless, in random samples differences between pairs of means of one variable correlate zero with differences between pairs of means of the other variable. Thus the formula for the multiple critical ratio (M.C.R.) is

$$\text{M.C.R.} = \frac{c_1 + c_2 + \cdots + c_m}{\sqrt{m}}.$$

Since there are several items common to the general adjustment scale and the morale scale, the combined critical ratio of 2.33 is excessive and somewhat spurious. When allowance is made for these factors, the combined critical ratio reduces to 1.7, or odds of about 9 to 1.

a difference, of the magnitude found, by pure chance? The odds are 49 to 1 of obtaining by chance a difference in pattern of adjustment as large as the advantage that the 80 WPA workers showed over a matched group of 42 direct-relief clients. Clearly, such a difference in pattern of social adjustment does not often occur by chance; therefore, we may conclude that the higher morale, general adjustment, social participation, and social status are probably due to the WPA program. In other words, we have some real evidence to support the conviction that a work program is better than direct relief in maintaining morale.

We must next try to answer such questions as the following: (1) Were the WPA group and the relief group studied selected groups that would show differences in morale anyway? (2) How can you know that the differences found were not due to other factors, since adjustment is at best a very complicated process? (3) What dependence can you put upon the measurements of morale; would not some other investigator have obtained a different result? (4) Can you rely for a description of differences in complex adjustment upon only four criteria, such as those used?

Consider the first question: (1) Were the WPA group and the relief group studied selected groups that would show differences in morale anyway? In March, 1939, when the study was begun, there were 8074 at work on WPA in St. Paul on the twenty-ninth of the month. At the same time there were only 465 cases in all on direct relief certified as employable and waiting assignment to WPA. Obviously, the number we had to choose from in the relief list was comparatively small. Our first step was to select a 5-per-cent sample at random from the WPA lists, to be compared with the direct-relief group. In order to simplify the problem of comparison, there were eliminated from the two samples all persons previously on WPA but now on the waiting list, all single persons, and all divorced, separated, and widowed cases. Also all persons not living in St. Paul and not working in Ramsey County were excluded. The result of equating the two groups, the WPA group and the direct-relief group, on these seven factors was to make all the individuals selected for study more comparable than would otherwise have been the case.

The next step was to eliminate from the two groups those individuals who still showed marked differences on other factors in addition to the seven mentioned above. Since marked differences in the distribution by former occupation, size of family, age, sex, years of education, race, and nativity might affect morale, the two groups were matched in respect to each of these seven additional factors. In this way, extreme variations were eliminated, and the two groups were made as similar as possible in all characteristics except morale and adjustment, which might be associated with being on WPA in one group and with receiving direct relief in the other. Thus our method of dealing with question (1) was to apply the familiar control-group procedure and so protect our results from the limitations that would arise from "selected" samples of "bias" in the groups to be compared. This process did, however, reduce the number of cases for interview, so that at the time the field work was begun, we had only 172 WPA and 102 relief cases, of which 130 WPA and 72 relief cases were interviewed.

Social workers and graduate students in social work then visited these persons in their homes and obtained from each person responses to the Rundquist-Sletto *Survey of Opinions* (from which the morale score and the general adjustment score of each individual was later computed) and also information on the *Social Participation Scale* and the *Social Status Scale*. In this process of interviewing additional cases were eliminated because of refusals, not located, moved out of town, changes in relief status, separated from relief, sickness and death, or working in private employment. The net result was the final groups, 80 WPA workers and 42 direct-relief clients, complete as to information on each of the four criteria used to measure adjustment and matched on 14 characteristic traits that were the ascertainable facts of their social situations (see Figure 3).

Turning now to the second question, (2) How can you know that the differences found were not due to other factors, since adjustment is at best a very complicated process? we can answer by stating that since we matched on seven initial factors (dwelling residence, work residence, previous WPA experience, single, divorced, separated, or widowed) and again on seven additional controlled factors (age, sex, size of family, former occupation, years of education, race, and nativity), the differences found in favor of WPA workers as compared with direct-relief clients could not have been due to these fourteen factors. Now it is apparent, of course, that factors upon which information was not obtainable could not be held constant by matching. Such factors will, no doubt, occur to the critical reader. All that we can say in extenuation is that we were limited by the available information and that another experiment

FIGURE 3.   Flow Chart of Process of Study

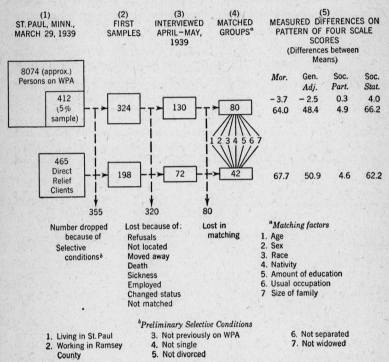

might be improved by more complete coverage. One such factor is income. This factor would have to be controlled if we desired a more precise isolation of the single factor, work, to determine how it alone is related to adjustment. Disparity of income as between the WPA and relief groups, otherwise matched on 14 factors, is not as serious a limitation as might first appear. In a previous study, we found that income tended to vary with the class of occupation and with the number of years of education. Consequently, when variation in occupation and variation in education were controlled, the variation in income was strikingly diminished. Since in the present WPA study we did control occupation and education, there is good reason to believe that income also was controlled to a marked extent. This evidence is indirect but is probably quite significant. Finally, it may be claimed with some point that larger income is a necessary part of the WPA program.

Another factor not controlled in obtaining the first results was length of time on relief.[11] By further elimination of cases in matched comparisons, we were able, however, to control this eighth factor.

TABLE 4.   Comparisons of the Morale, General Adjustment, Social Participation, and Social Status Between WPA Workers and Relief Clients, Holding Constant Sex, Race, Nativity, Usual Occupation, Age, Education, Size of Family, and Length of Time on Relief

Groups Compared, Differences and Constants	Variables Compared			
	Morale [a]	General Adjustment [a]	Social Participation	Social Status
Means				
1. WPA group ($n = 37$)....	65.27	49.54	5.19	62.78
2. Relief group ($n = 25$)....	66.76	50.44	5.84	59.44
Differences between means	−1.49	−0.90	−0.65	+3.34
Critical ratios (Fisher's formula)..............	−0.56	−0.46	−0.32	+0.47

[a] Lower morale and adjustment scores on the Rundquist-Sletto test indicate higher morale and adjustment in the customary meaning of these terms.

This process reduced the final numbers to 37 WPA and 25 direct-relief cases. In this final comparison the WPA group still showed a better pattern of adjustment on the whole than the relief group, although the absolute differences on each of the four measures of

[11] Time on relief means here the length of time since the subject's family was registered for the first time with the direct-relief agency. All WPA workers in St. Paul were so registered before being placed on WPA projects.

adjustment were smaller than in the case of comparisons using seven controlled factors [12] (see Table 4).

The next question now deserves attention: (3) What dependence can you put upon the measurements of morale; would not some other investigator have obtained a different result? The answer to this question is the simplest of the list. It is this: Morale was measured by responses to a standardized scale constructed to measure morale. By a standardized scale we mean a measuring instrument that has been tested hundreds of times and does, in fact, give almost identical results when used by different investigators on the same or similar groups of subjects. Thus, the morale scale is a reliable scale. It is also a valid scale. It does measure what it is designed to measure because it differentiates employed and unemployed persons and other contrasting groups which are ordinarily taken as typical of differences in morale by common-sense judgments of competent persons. The same conditions of reliability and validity are met by the other three scales: general adjustment, social participation, and social status.

Since the critical reader may wish to know additional facts about the method of using these four scales in interviews, the following description may anticipate further questions.

The scales measure: (1) *morale,* or the degree that the individual feels competent to cope with the future and to achieve his desired goals; (2) *general adjustment,* or the feelings about his relationship to other persons, toward present or future social conditions, and toward present social institutions; (3) *social participation,* or the degree to which an individual actually engages in the organized activities of his community in terms of membership, attendance, contributions, committees, and offices; and (4) *social status,* or the position the family occupies with reference to the average prevailing household possessions of other families in the community.

It will be noted that the scales to measure morale and general adjustment describe *how people feel* about their situation, whereas the scales that measure social participation and social status de-

[12] These decreases in differences probably reflected fluctuations, owing to the small number of cases in these samples remaining after adding time on relief as a control.

scribe their *objective social condition*. Together, the four scales enable us to describe the pattern of their adjustment to new or to old surroundings. Since each scale has been in use and tested out hundreds of times in a number of social investigations, there are published norms available for comparison. For example, morale scores of 58 to 59 points obtained from slum populations in another 1939 study are decidedly better than 65 for WPA and 67 for relief clients studied at the same time (see Table 3) and not far from those of the normal population. The general adjustment scores of 43 points in the same slum study are similarly better than 49 for the WPA and 50 for relief clients, and again not far from those of the normal population. The participation scores of the WPA and relief clients are worse than those of slum families in a previous study of the same area. Social status scores of 57 and 59 points in the same slum study compare unfavorably with those of the WPA (63) and of the relief group (59). Previous studies show, however, that a score in the fifties is within the observed range of normal working-class families in Minneapolis, Massachusetts, and Alabama.

The material gathered in the interview consisted of:

Minnesota Survey of Opinions, two sheets with 31 questions about the individual's attitudes, to be filled in by the subject. After the interview, the *moral score* and the *general adjustment score* may be extracted from the subject's marked response by a simple system of weighing and scoring. It takes the subject from 20 to 30 minutes to fill this in.[13]

Social Participation Scale, one sheet for entries on each group affiliation of subject recorded in five entries under five columns by the visitor in reply to questions answered by the subject. It takes 10 or 15 minutes to fill in the subject's answers.[14]

Social Status Scale, one sheet containing 21 entries filled in as observations made by the visitor, with perhaps one or two non-inquisitorial questions. Can be completed in 5 minutes' observation.

[13] These scales and their norms will be found in E. A. Rundquist and R. F. Sletto, *Personality in the Depression,* University of Minnesota Press, 1936.

[14] These scales and their norms will be found in F. S. Chapin, *Contemporary American Institutions,* Harper & Brothers, 1935, and 1946 ed., reprinted by William C. Brown, Dubuque, Ia., pp. 373–397; and F. S. Chapin, "Social Participation and Social Intelligence," *American Sociological Review,* April, 1939, pp. 157–166.

Finally, the reader may ask question (4), Can you rely for a description of differences in complex adjustment upon only four criteria, such as those used? This is a difficult question and only a qualified answer can be given, an answer which the reader may accept or not, according to his own judgment. The answer can be made only in terms of several considerations. In the first place, the four scales have differentiated between Negroes and Jews in a slum population study in Minneapolis in 1935–1936, between overcrowded slum families and not overcrowded slum families,[15] and between former Boy Scouts of four-year tenure and Boy Scouts with two-year tenure in 1938.[16] In the second place, the probability of a chance difference in pattern of adjustment between WPA workers and direct-relief clients is 49 against 1, whereas the highest chance occurrence for any single criterion (morale) is one in which the odds are only 17 to 1. Obviously, a pattern of differences on four factors (morale, general adjustment, social participation, and social status) is less likely to occur by chance in random sampling than is a difference on any single factor. Hence when such a difference in pattern does occur, we may conclude that it probably represents a real difference between the WPA and direct-relief groups studied.[17]

The chief purpose of this study was to discover whether a better

[15] F. S. Chapin, "The Effects of Slum Clearance on Family and Community Relationships in Minneapolis in 1935–1936," *American Journal of Sociology*, March, 1938, pp. 744–763.

[16] N. G. Mandel, "A Controlled Analysis of the Relationship of Boy Scout Tenure and Participation in Community Adjustment," M.A. thesis, University of Minnesota, July, 1938; and preceding section in this chapter.

[17] The differences in favor of WPA workers found in this study were obtained several weeks before the strikes of July, 1939, and so could not have been influenced by these disturbances. Utmost care was taken to allay suspicion by making it clear at the beginning of each interview that we were asking cooperation in obtaining people's opinions as part of a larger study conducted by a sociologist at the University of Minnesota. It was made clear that this study had no bearing on WPA operations. Although the results of this study are favorable to the WPA program in St. Paul as of the spring of 1939, every precaution was taken to secure objectivity and to avoid bias. Although the WPA Division of Research expressed an interest in the results, the collection and interpretation of the facts were carried out entirely by us without suggestions or restrictions, except concerning administrative matters related to the use of WPA official records. Under these circumstances the discovery of results favorable to WPA is all the more significant.

adjustment of WPA workers than a comparable group of direct-relief clients could be established as caused by the Works program. The outcome of this single and somewhat limited study does establish the probability of such a cause-and-effect relationship. Social workers are justly skeptical of simple cause-and-effect explanations in the complex social life of today. It is wisely observed that a large number of influences combine to explain each specific social situation. And yet, by matched groupings, we have succeeded in securing some control over fourteen factors related to the etiology of individual adjustment. When these fourteen factors are held constant, we discover that in St. Paul the Works program is associated with higher adjustment and direct relief is associated with lower adjustment. We cannot arbitrarily say whether the absolute differences found on measures of adjustment are important. We can and do state that there is a slight probability against the chance occurrence of absolute differences of the magnitudes actually found. When we say "chance," we mean a large number of small causes; for "chance" is a term which never means, in the language of science, the absence of cause. When the odds are heavy against a difference being due to chance (i.e., due to many small influences or causes), then we may claim that the differences are probably due to a few very influential factors, or causes, in this case the WPA program as contrasted to the direct-relief program.

How far these favorable results from the 1939 St. Paul study may be generalized to WPA at large, it is not possible to state. Obviously, the next step is to extend this sort of study to other areas, repeat the procedures, and discover if the results are verified or disproved.

In passing from this chapter to a description of projected experimental design in Chapter IV, and to ex post facto experimental design in Chapter V, we make a transition from analysis of association between two factors at one date to the method of controlled observation of changes in this association that occur over an interval of time. Here we make the attempt to discover the type of association that is called cause and effect, or concomitant variation.

Chapter IV

PROJECTED EXPERIMENTAL DESIGN. THE CLASSICAL PATTERN OF "BEFORE" AND "AFTER" EXPERIMENTS THAT OPERATE FROM THE PRESENT TO THE FUTURE

AMELIORATION of the problems of human relations often takes the form of social programs of treatment to achieve desired ends. But interwoven with the means or the social programs to attain chosen objectives there are other individual and social factors which combine to effect the results. The method of projected experimental design provides a technique of study which we believe will enable us, as the technique is improved, to separate the planned means-ends schema from the more impersonal cause-effect relationships, so that we may assign some measure of relative influence to each. It is the purpose of this chapter to analyze four studies: the effects of a program of rural hygiene in Syria; the social effects of public housing in Minneapolis; the results of a student counseling program at the University of Wisconsin; and the consequences of a program of social treatment on juvenile delinquents in New York City. Before examining these separate studies, a brief consideration of the concept of cause and effect seems indicated.[1]

---

[1] An extensive treatment of the concept will be found in R. M. MacIver's *Social Causation*, Ginn, 1942, and R. B. Lindsay's article, "Causality in the Physical World," *Scientific Monthly*, October, 1933, pp. 330–337, is an excellent brief summary. The concept of prediction is closely related to the concept of causation. The former was discussed in chap. 1 of this book, especially in its semantic connotations. For an extended discussion see Paul Horst *et al., The Prediction of Personal Adjustment*, Bulletin 48, Social Science Research Council, 1941. It is desirable to distinguish between the concept of estimation and the concept of prediction. The former relates to the calculation of values of a dependent variable by substitution in a regression equation of the successive values of the independent variable or variables and does not necessarily include the time factor, which is a fundamental element in the concept of prediction.

Cause and effect, or causality as a system of ideas, is an explanation of successive events by a set of assumed antecedent-consequent relationships for which the evidence is objective and recurrent. In the area of physical things this type of explanation is quite generally accepted as a true explanation of what happens. In fact, predictions can be made with considerable confidence in narrow areas of experience, and in mechanics, where control is quite complete, determinism reigns. But in the area of human relations explanations of social events in terms of cause and effect have made only crude beginnings, and more often than not are rejected as entirely inapplicable. But let us consider the alternatives.

The alternatives to acceptance of the causality explanation of human relations are to accept: (1) chaos; (2) magic, demonism, and supernaturalism; or (3) means-ends explanations. Since chaos is no explanation at all, but a confession of the permanence of ignorance and of the persistence of impotence, it has to be discarded in any effort at rational explanation of social relations. Similarly, magic, demonism, metaphysics, and supernaturalism have failed to explain the problems of social relations in a rational manner, albeit such systems of thought still, unfortunately, influence human relations. Even the means-ends explanation is only a partial answer to our questions, since many social events, like inflation, a run on a bank, and world war, defy explanation in the simple terms of purpose, design, and planning by any single or preponderate means-ends schema. Nevertheless it is perfectly evident that narrowly conceived means-ends schemata do produce social effects, as when labor unions resort to strike to better the working conditions of their members, or when huge industries plan to achieve monopoly. But the situation is not so simple in other cases. When different interest groups in a community pursue their own independent means-ends plans without regard for consequences to the larger public, there are unplanned results that come from the combinations of these independently planned social actions. Such seems to be the case in the problem of inflation, and for the global community this is the case in the problem of world wars. Although the causal explanation of the problems of inflation and of world wars is now based upon insufficient knowledge of the many factors at work, it does have the advantage of a courageous effort to seek understanding which strives on the one hand to avoid escape from reality into phantasy and chaos, and on the other hand to avoid yielding to the blandishments of magic, demonism, and supernaturalism. The concept of causality when frankly empirical helps to order our thinking about complex problems to a logical system susceptible of test by facts.

The Concept of Causality: Cause and Effect

The concept of cause and effect as used in this book, therefore, does not mean rigid determinism. Rather it is used as a shorthand device to represent a kind of association between factors in time sequence which has a determinable probability of occurrence. Cause and effect is useful terminology since it is a more objectifiable mode of verbal expression than the folk language concept of means-ends. In the case of means and ends we are concerned primarily with preferred means to attain objectives that are desired.

By substituting the concept of cause and effect we avoid undue emphasis on the function of language to *express feeling* and emotion by turning attention to its *representative function*. This is achieved by resort to observation of how things happen. Is the factor X (treatment) associated with the factor Y (adjustment)? This is a question that can be answered by correlation analysis once we have developed reliable scales to measure degrees of treatment and degrees of adjustment, that is, quantitative description of X and Y. The next step is to find out whether X precedes Y by an interval of time that can be described in the operations of measurement. When we find that changes in the magnitude of Y (measured adjustment), between a date when X (treatment) was begun and a second date when treatment was terminated, are changes in magnitude which occur very infrequently in chance, or in the fluctuations of random samples (the control group) selected from a non-treated universe of persons in other respects similar to those receiving treatment, we conclude that a calculable degree of probability supports the hypothesis that extended treatment causes changes in personal adjustment.

Thus defined, in terms of operations performed, to describe how events happen, an element of objectivity is introduced into our procedure, i.e., two or more equally competent observers may check one another's records because the terms used in describing what happens represent differences in kind or preferably of degree (measurement on a scale) of attributes (treatment and adjustment) of the subjects studied; and the terms do not express merely how the observer *feels* about that which he observes. We fall into the latter situation when our account of treatment states that an appeal to the better nature of a delinquent boy can and does lead to an improvement in his conduct. By using such words as "better" and "improvement" we disclose the fact that the observer has an emotional set or belief or preference for certain forms of behavior or states of being as against others. The objection to the latter type of verbal expression is the difficulty of obtaining agreement on the meaning of "better" or "improvement" *after* these terms have been used. When we substitute for these normative terms the concept of change in mean score on a reliable scale that measures adjustment,[2] we have a statement that can be verified, since equally competent observers using the same scale on the same subjects under the same conditions would obtain results differing only in terms of small errors of observation, the frequency of which would tend to occur in approximation to some probability distribution. Thus the purpose of "before" and "after" measurements is to supply an operation which adds to the objectivity of description; it is not a commitment to an assumption of rigid determinism.

[2] This is the question of validity of the scale, and we assume that the scale in question discriminates between individuals in degrees that are consistent with some independent criterion of the same attribute. But even *before* validation of the completed scale as above, an element of validity is introduced when the component items of the proposed scale are rated independently by judges whose opinions are generally accepted in the community as discriminating judgments, thus providing an initial agreement on the meaning of items, a procedure in sharp contrast to that in which statements of interested practitioners who are working on the case are taken at their face value.

THE EFFECTS OF RURAL HYGIENE IN SYRIA

One of the best documented and recorded results of an experiment that has been published is Stuart C. Dodd's, *A Controlled Experiment on Rural Hygiene in Syria*.[3] Dodd set out to discover the relationship between a program of rural hygiene and the hygienic practices of the families that were supposed to benefit by the program. The program of education in hygiene was put on by an itinerant traveling clinic of the Near East Foundation from 1931 to 1933. The beneficiaries were 40 families in the Arab village of Jib Ramli in Syria. It is generally believed that efforts to improve the hygienic practices of individuals and families actually result in such improvement that morbidity and mortality are lowered, and general comfort and happiness is increased. Strange as it may seem, the validity of this assumption has seldom been tested, although millions of dollars are spent annually throughout the world on preventive medicine.

Dodd decided to set up an experiment that would attempt to measure the effects of hygienic education upon the hygienic practices of a group of individuals and families. In his study, "Hygiene means all the knowledge, practices, and environmental conditions which are under the control of the family and which tend to increase health."[4] To determine the progress in hygiene, it was necessary to measure change in hygiene in the direction desired by the groups undergoing it. Observe that there is no arbitrary or absolute goal to be attained. The goal is one determined by the opinions of the people. The scale to measure hygienic change was, however, constructed in an objective manner and its reliability and validity were determined. A preliminary list of 270 questions was scored on a 1000-point scale with the assistance of nine competent judges who allocated the weights. From this list, a shorter form of 77 significant questions was derived.[5] Sources of error were examined and shown

[3] Publications of the Faculty of Arts and Sciences, *Social Science Series*, No. 7, American University of Beirut, 1934, pp. 336 ff.

[4] *Ibid.*, p. xii.

[5] *Ibid.*, p. 57.

not to exist as between samples, different informants in one family, different interviewers, and different scorers. Reliability coefficients of + .91 on informants and + .94 on interviewers were found. Validity coefficients of + .76 were obtained with indices of mortality or "survival," of − .53 with morbidity, and of + .65 with longevity.[6]

The scale to measure hygiene having been standardized, the next problem was to select villages to serve as controls on the experimental village that received instruction. Three Arab villages were selected as controls although only one survived the test as an adequate control. These villages were located so that there was little likelihood of hygienic practices spreading to them from the experimental village of Jib Ramli. They were selected also with reference to their similarity both to the experimental village and among themselves on nine different factors which, if variable, might themselves explain the final effect, rather than the final effect being the result of the program of instruction in hygiene. The controlled variables were: geographic, demographic, historical, economic, religious, domestic, educational, recreational, and sanitary conditions. The extent to which these controls were quantitatively established is not clear.

In 1931, all four villages were scored on the hygiene scale. Then for two years, that is, from 1931 to 1933, the experimental village of Jib Ramli received systematic instruction by visits from the traveling clinic. The control villages received no such instruction and were by geographic location supposed to be isolated from any influence spreading from the clinic. In 1933, all four villages were again measured on the same hygiene scale and their scores compared. It was found that the experimental village increased its score from 253 points in 1931 to 304 points in 1933, a gain of 51 points, at the close of the period of hygiene instruction. The control village also increased its score, from 241 points in 1931 to 286 points in 1933, a gain of 45 points without visible instruction in hygiene. Does the fact that the experimental village gained six points more than the control village prove that the effects of a hygiene program are less marked than is generally believed? Dodd makes no such claim. He concludes that the experiment may have been vitiated by incomplete isolation of the control village from the influences of

[6] *Ibid.*, p. 82.

the clinic.[7] Our opinion is that an additional weakness in the experiment was the inability to obtain adequate control of the nine factors supposedly held constant.

This example of the application of the experimental method to the study of a socio-educational problem is valuable in three ways: first, it is an admirable demonstration of the technique of constructing a scale of measurement in a difficult field of individual behavior; second, it is a clean-cut demonstration of the pattern of an experimental setup; and third, the results are allowed to speak for themselves, with critical comments by the experimenter on the weaknesses of his experiment. To prove the relationship between instruction in hygiene and progress in hygiene, similar experiments are required. In other words, a sociological experiment demonstrates the existence of a postulated relationship only after it has been repeated a number of times and its results have been verified. The significance of this statement should not be lost. Note that we have said, "after it has been repeated a number of times and its results have been verified." Reproducibility and verifiability are qualities of scientific observation that the experimental method supplies to the sociologist who is patient enough to do the hard work extending over months or years, and willing to stay by his research until he secures results that can have wide acceptance.

But to return to the Dodd experiment, it is evident that the crucial problem was that of controlling the variables in the situation under investigation. Since the heart of the experimental method is the observation of the relationship of two variables when all others are controlled, it is evident that failure to control these other variables vitiates or at least obscures the results. In 1931, we published a paper, "The Problem of Controls in Experimental Sociology,"[8] in which the various techniques of control then used were analyzed on the basis of several published experimental studies. Since the publication of the Dodd experiment, the problem of controls again comes to the front as a crucial problem which, if unsolved, is likely to hold back the application of experimental method to the study of social relationships.

[7] Ibid., p. xiv.
[8] Journal of Educational Sociology, May, 1931.

THE SOCIAL EFFECTS OF PUBLIC HOUSING IN MINNEAPOLIS

Is the condition of a slum family improved by rehousing in a model public housing project? An affirmative answer to this question is assumed as the justification for the expenditure of millions of dollars. Is there any proof of this assumption aside from common-sense expectation?

This study is an effort to measure the effects of good housing upon former slum families rehoused in Sumner Field Homes of Minneapolis, originally a project of the Housing Division of the PWA and since 1937 under the management of the FPHA.

The most interesting findings of this study are: (1) No significant change in morale or in general adjustment was found in 1940 as compared to 1939, either for the 44 experimental families resident in the project, or for the control group of 38 families residing in the slum; (2) both the resident and control groups gained in social participation from 1939 to 1940, but the resident families gained twice as much in absolute score as the control group; (3) both resident and control groups gained in social status from 1939 to 1940, but the residents showed a gain of greater magnitude; (4) a score made on the "condition of the furnishings of the living room" showed for the residents a striking gain but for the control group a real loss for the 12-month period; and (5) both residents and control group had improved in the percentage of families "use-crowded" in 1940 over 1939, but the gain of the residents was about three times that of the control group.

Thus the improvements in condition accrue in much larger degree to the residents of the project, and seem to justify the housing program in so far as the facts of this single study are concerned.

Before examining the evidence that supports the foregoing conclusions, it may be helpful to analyze the causal components in the complex of factors which operate in the social situation of slum dwelling compared with public housing, as well as to consider the factors chosen to measure the patterns of response to these differences in housing.

In the first place, since the purpose of this experimental study was to discover the results of public housing, we may interpret the results as ends achieved in a means-ends schema of social reform, or we may interpret the results as the effects of multiple causation by impersonal factors. Results are ends achieved when a rule of public housing prevents room-crowding by limits placed on dwelling unit occupancy, and also when a social program results in the organization of clubs and recreational groups among public housing tenants.

On the other hand, public housing standards for interior space and lighting, reduction of noise transmission by structural standards, and regulations for safety and sanitation combine as impersonal factors in a complex of causes which result in greater measured cleanliness, orderliness, and neatness in the living room of the home, as well as a diminished percentage of use-crowding, and encourage indoor entertainment and recreation which, in turn, are expressed in higher social participation scores.

The assertion has been made that housing per se, the intrinsic housing factor, cannot be defined or measured. It may be submitted that housing per se is a combination of many factors, such as adequate space and light, reduced noise, room-crowding prevention, and provision for indoor entertainment and recreation, safety and sanitation. The response of tenants to different degrees of this pattern of intrinsic housing factors may be observed and measured by the score on the condition of living rooms, the score on social participation, and the percentage use-crowded, all three showing differences before and after public housing, as compared with continuous slum dwelling.

But these specific factors, whether they be regarded as a program of means or as a causal complex, do not exhaust the list of influences at work. There are always present status factors such as the state of employment, differences in education and in income, various occupational groups, etc.; and biological factors, such as the size of family and racial differences (which operate not as intrinsic biological differences but as biological variations which lead to social factors such as exclusion and segregation). Then, too, there are known but unmeasured factors such as differences in the state of health and in habits of household economy. Last of all there are many unknown factors. All of these may operate to obscure the real effect of differences in the causal pattern of intrinsic housing factors.

In summary, and in the interests of clarity of thought about this complex problem of chosen means to desired ends or of causal factors antecedent to the effect, we may list the foregoing housing influences as:

M. The means
    1. Occupancy rules
    2. Social program
H. Housing influences per se
    3. Space
    4. Light
    5. Noise
    6. Room-crowding
    7. Indoor provision for entertainment and recreation
    8. Safety
    9. Sanitation
S. Status factors (obscuring M and H)
    10. Employment
    11. Education
    12. Income
    13. Occupation
B. Biological factors
    14. Size of family
    15. Race
U. (1) Unmeasured factors
    16. Health
    17. Habits of household economy
U. (2) Unknown factors

Measures of Results

In studies by experimental design of the social effects of housing, we need to decide in advance of the investigation upon some measures of effect or some means of appraising the degree to which the desired end has been achieved. In this connection it is advisable to meet certain conditions as follows:

1. Scales used to measure effect should be reliable and valid instruments of observation and numerical description (see Chapter VI, pp. 152–154).

2. Scales that have been used in previous studies of the same problem or a similar problem and have yielded norms on the same kind of population to be studied are valuable for comparisons, and should be chosen for use.

3. These scales should, of course, measure traits or responses that will be accepted as indices of effect or as indices of the degree to which the desired end has been achieved. The scales should, in short, measure traits or responses that are relevant to the problem.

4. Such scales will be even more useful if we have prior knowledge of whether they are correlated with certain known causal variables —variables other than the complex of factors which have been selected as the means to the end desired, or the assumed cause of the effect to be studied—because this facilitates control of these disturbing factors by matching on measurements (see Appendices A and B).

5. Finally, the scales will be still more serviceable if it can be shown that they measure a *bundle* of interrelated traits that emerge as a *pattern of response* to the particular treatment or program which is the causal complex to be evaluated in terms of its results.

All these conditions are met in some degree for an experimental study of the social effects of housing if the three following measures are used: scale on the condition of the living room (see pp. 76–77, also Appendix A); percentage of dwelling units that are use-crowded; and the social participation scale (see Appendix B). The evidence for this assertion will now be considered.

1. The scale on *the condition of the living room* of a dwelling unit has shown reliability coefficients as high as $r = .95$, despite its appearance of subjectivity of estimate, and validity coefficients of bis. $r = .45$ with use-crowding, and of $r = .52$ with the deficiency rating obtained by use of the *Appraisal Form* of the Committee on Hygiene of Housing (condition 1); it is a scale that has been used in several studies of many low-income families living in slum areas of the Twin Cities (condition 2); it supplies an objective measure

of such qualitative traits as cleanliness, orderliness, and condition of repair of articles and furnishings in a living room (condition 3); it shows different mean scores for different income classes and different occupational groups in an urban community, and rises from 3.9 for unskilled and semi-skilled occupational groups to 6.4 for managerial and professional groups, of a representative sample of an urban community, so that, by matching on income and occupation, that part of its variation not due to housing, but due to status factors, may be partially controlled (condition 4); and finally, it has been found related to use-crowding by bis. $r = .45$. Scores on the condition of the living room of a dwelling are obtained from part II of the *Social Status Scale* cited below.

2. The percentage of dwelling units that are *use-crowded* is a measure of the multiple use of the rooms of a dwelling. When a bedroom (BR) is used also as a dining room (DR), or a kitchen (K) is used also as a living room (LR), the situation is called use-crowded. The following multiple uses of rooms originally designed to serve only one function represent degrees of use-crowding with appropriate penalties expressed numerically for purposes of measurement: LR and DR (-6); LR and K (-9); LR and BR (-12) or DR and K (-12); LR and BR and DR and K (-15). Such situational uses distort and confuse the functions of living. Thus the incidence and degree of use-crowding is taken as an index of undesirable housing and is an index quite different from, but related to, room-crowding, or the number of persons per room in the dwelling unit. Use-crowding is a sensitive measure of housing adequacy.

3. *Social participation,* or the number of clubs, formal social groups, organizations, or societies, that the persons in the family are active in, or members of, is related to provisions for indoor entertainment of visitors and to the recreation of individuals in the home. Social participation has been measured by a simple scale which obtains a total score on any person as follows: one point counted for each group membership; two points counted for each group that is attended; three points counted for each group to which some financial contribution is made; four points counted for each committee membership held; and five points counted for each of-

ficial position held, such as secretary, treasurer, president, etc. This social participation scale has shown reliability coefficients of from $r = .88$ to $r = .95$, and validity coefficients of from $r = .52$ to $r = .62$ (condition 1); it has been used to measure the social activities in formal groups of the community in urban areas of both low social status and high social status, and tentative norms are available to show the mean scores obtained for different income classes and occupational groups (see Appendix B), and for both sexes (condition 2); social participation is relevant to housing since most public housing programs encourage clubs and social activities (condition 3); social participation scores have been found to be correlated with income, $r = .36$ to $.49$, with occupational group, $r = .31$ to $.56$, and with years of formal education, $r = .33$ to $.44$. For these reasons it is evident that by matching on education, income, and occupation, that part of any change in social participation score due to such non-housing factors as education, income, and occupation may be partially controlled (condition 4); finally, an attractive living room, not used also for eating, or cooking, or sleeping purposes, is a place in which club meetings may be comfortably held, and so social participation in the home may be related to measures of use-crowding and the condition of the living room.

Since the three measures just described were shown to be inter-related in ways expressed as correlation coefficients or by other empirical evidence, they satisfy condition 5. Furthermore, the use of the multiple critical ratio, which combines critical ratios on each of the separate measures, yields results that have high statistical significance for the results in the housing study herein described—additional evidence that condition 5 has been met.

The study was planned in 1938 to test the hypothesis: the rehousing of slum families in a public housing project results in improvement of the living conditions and the social life of these families. Sumner Field Homes was selected as the test case. In an earlier study of 1935–1936, we reported on the immediate effects of slum clearance and temporary rehousing of 171 slum families.[9] The pres-

[9] F. Stuart Chapin, "The Effects of Slum Clearance and Re-housing on Families and Community Relationships in Minneapolis," *American Journal of Sociology,* March, 1938, pp. 744–763.

ent study is, therefore, a follow-up conducted upon a more systematic and experimental procedure. To test the hypothesis of improvement, we selected 108 project families (1939) as the experimental group and 131 families in slum neighborhoods as the control group.

The experimental group of resident families were those admitted to the project after December 16, 1938. The families in the control group were living in the slum and were chosen from the "waiting list," i.e., from the group of applicants fully investigated by the USHA agents but not immediately accepted as residents because they lived in poor housing not definitely sub-standard, or their income was uncertain, or there was some question of economic or social stability. They remained as eligible rejects or deferred cases for later reconsideration provided subsequent applicants did not meet the requirements in sufficient numbers to fill up the project. There were about 603 families in the waiting list. For the reasons given, they were a group comparable to residents. The control group of slum families was 21.3 per cent larger than the experimental group of residents to allow for shrinkage due to moving away, refusals, or other reasons.

How can we measure the effects of good housing? Are residents of the project better adjusted than slum residents? The attempt to measure the effects of good housing utilized four sociometric scales that have been applied successfully in other previous studies: a slum family study in Minneapolis in 1935–1936,[10] and a WPA relief study in St. Paul in 1939.[11]

The scales measure: (1) *morale,* or the degree that the individual *feels* competent to cope with the future and to achieve his desired goals; (2) *general adjustment,* or the *feelings* about his relationship to other persons, toward present or future social conditions, and toward present social institutions; (3) *social participation,* or the degree to which an individual *actually* engages in the organized

[10] *Ibid.*
[11] F. Stuart Chapin and Julius A. Jahn, "The Advantages of Work Relief over Direct Relief in Maintaining Morale in St. Paul in 1939," *American Journal of Sociology,* July, 1940, pp. 13–22. See also chap. III, pp. 41–50.

activities of his community in terms of membership, attendance, contributions, committees, and offices; and (4) *social status,* or the position the family occupies with reference to the average prevailing household possessions of other families in the community.

Interviewing of residents and non-residents began in February, 1939, and continued intermittently through July, 1939, when a total of 239 had been interviewed, 108 residents and 131 non-residents. A group of 12 interviewers, graduate students in sociology and social work at the University of Minnesota, made the interviews. Only two were paid; the remainder were volunteers. The visitors were instructed in a group meeting and each was provided with sheets of typed directions before going into the field. Entree to the families was obtained by the visitor's stating that he was collecting information about people's opinions as part of a wider study being made under the direction of a university scientist. No mention was made of any connection of this study with the USHA. In this way it was felt that a more spontaneous response would be obtained. The interview furnished the following data.

Minnesota Survey of Opinions, two sheets with 31 questions about the individual's attitudes, to be filled in by the subject. After the interview, the *morale score* and the *general adjustment score* may be extracted from the subject's marked response by a simple system of weighting and scoring. It takes the subject from 20 to 30 minutes to fill this in.[12]

Social Participation Scale, one sheet for entries on each group affiliation of subject recorded in five entries under five columns by the visitor in reply to questions answered by the subject. It takes 10 or 15 minutes to fill in the subject's answers.[13]

Social Status Scale, one sheet containing 21 entries filled in as observations made by the visitor, with perhaps one or two non-inquisitorial questions. Can be completed in 5 minutes' observation.[13]

[12] These scales and their norms will be found in E. A. Rundquist and R. F. Sletto, *Personality in the Depression,* University of Minnesota Press, 1936.

[13] These scales and their norms will be found in F. S. Chapin, *Contemporary American Institutions,* Harper & Brothers, 1935, and W. C. Brown, 1946, pp. 373–397; and F. S. Chapin, "Social Participation and Social Intelligence," *American Sociological Review,* April, 1939, pp. 157–166.

The flow chart illustrates the actual shrinkage from the initial group of 108 resident families to the final group of 44 resident families, and from the initial group of 131 slum families not resident in the project (called the control group) to the final group of 38 families. At each step in the study, the elimination of families is shown in the flow chart with the reason for this.

The 103 resident families and the 88 non-resident families that were interviewed in 1939 were matched on the following factors:

1. Race or cultural class of husband (Negro, Jew, mixed white)
2. Employment of husband (private, unemployed, OAA, WPA)
3. Occupational class of husband (I-professional, II-managerial, III-clerical, etc., using the Minnesota Rating Scale of occupations)
4. Number of persons in the family (2, 2–3, 3–5, etc.)
5. Income of the family ($690–814, 815–939, etc.)

When so matched, the results of interviewing to obtain scores on morale and on general adjustment, as well as scores on social participation and social status, showed the two groups to be very much alike. In fact, none of the critical ratios of the absolute differences in scores were statistically significant and in all cases were — 1.01 or less. This result establishes the fact that the initial experimental group and the initial control group matched on five factors began the experiment in 1939 (visiting was from February 1 to July 31) with a common base or zero point from which to measure change or gains.

Five additional matching factors were then added because it was found that the responses on the morale and general adjustment scales were made chiefly by housewives. These five factors were:

6. Race or cultural class of wife
7. Employment of wife
8. Occupational class of wife
9. Age of wife (16–20, 21–30, etc.)
10. Years education of wife (1–4, 5–8, etc.)

This process eliminated 47 cases from the experimental group of residents, and 12 cases from the control group of non-residents for the reasons shown on the flow chart. This brought us to the end

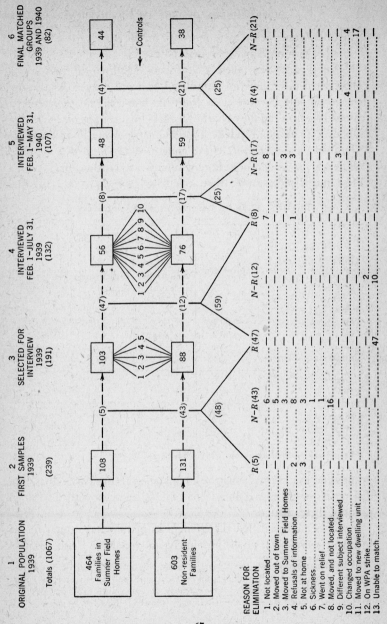

FIGURE 4. Flow Chart of Effects of Good Housing in Minneapolis, 1939-1940

67

of the 1939 study with measurements on 56 cases of residents and 76 cases of non-residents or controls.

The next step was taken a year later (February 1 to May 31, 1940), when the follow-up eliminated 12 more cases from the resident group and 38 more cases from the non-resident group for the reasons listed on the flow chart. This left final groups of 44 resident families and 38 non-resident families matched on 10 factors. The 38 families were *occupants of the same dwelling unit in 1939 and in 1940*. This also added one more constant matching factor.[14]

The mean scores were then calculated for these two matched

TABLE 5.   Measured Changes Associated with Housing

Groups Compared	Means of Measures of Effect			
	Morale [a] Scores	General [a] Adjustment Scores	Social Participation Scores	Social Status Scores
Residents (N = 44)				
1939	60.1	45.0	1.73	60.5
1940	60.2	44.0	6.34	86.7
Change	0.1	−1.0	4.61	26.2
Critical ratio of change	0.12	−0.97	3.69	4.27
Non-residents (N = 38)				
1939	58.0	42.4	2.76	61.1
1940	56.6	41.2	4.87	82.2
Change	−1.4	−1.2	2.11	21.1
Critical ratio of change	−1.28	−1.34	2.88	3.82

[a] Reverse scales, hence minus change interpreted as a gain.

groups and the 1939 values were compared with the 1940 values. The differences or gains are shown in Table 5, together with the critical ratios of these changes.

It will be observed that the changes in morale and in general adjustment were very small, absolutely and relatively, and that the

---

[14] All things considered, there were in reality 13 constants: the 10 factors enumerated above; the same dwelling unit at each date; and, since scores on *general adjustment* and *morale* remained approximately the same, they may be regarded as 2 additional control factors, although initially chosen as measures of effect.

critical ratios of these changes show them to be not statistically significant (that is, less than 2). On the other hand, the measured changes in social participation and in social status were large in absolute magnitude and were statistically significant. This observation applies with special emphasis to the residents, who gained more in magnitude and with statistically significant gains.

There are two explanations of the insignificant changes in morale and in general adjustment. First, when the raw scores on morale and general adjustment of Table 5 are converted into standard scores by the Rundquist-Sletto tables,[15] it appears that the morale and general adjustment of these housewives of slum families were about at the level of the normal population. Since they were evidently not depressed or variant, it was to be expected that a change in residence for one year would have only slight effect. Second, the morale and general adjustment scores of the experimental group in 1939 were obtained *after* occupancy of a dwelling unit in the housing project, so that if any gain had been experienced in relation to improved housing, it would have taken place earlier. The *Survey of Opinions* form which yielded the scores on morale and on general adjustment was not part of the interviews conducted by agents of the USHA when making an initial investigation of applicants, since to have included this additional form would have increased the time of interview beyond the limit thought to be appropriate by the USHA; consequently, we were obliged to use this *Survey of Opinions* form in later interviews made by graduate student and social work visitors as described above. However, all of the social participation and social status scores, as well as the information as to percentage of families use-crowded, were obtained as part of the initial interviews made by the USHA visitors, and include all of the 1067 families in 1939. The 1940 information on all scales was obtained by graduate students and social workers.[16] Since the changes measured

15 Rundquist and Sletto, *op. cit.,* pp. 389–391.

16 A year is perhaps only a short time for changes in morale and in general adjustment to register. The very slight gain on these measures shown by the nonresidents reflects perhaps the improvement in economic conditions and in general prosperity. Data on total unduplicated public welfare case count for Minneapolis show a substantial improvement in 1940 over 1939. The index of store sales of the

on morale and general adjustment were so indeterminate, our re-maining argument will be based upon the substantial changes in (a) social participation, (b) condition of furnishings in the living room, and (c) percentage of families in each group use-crowded.

Let us now turn to a systematic consideration of the factual evidence to discover how far it supports our original hypothesis. As stated on page 63, this hypothesis was: "The rehousing of slum families in a public housing project results in improvement of the living conditions and the social life of these families."

This positive form of the hypothesis has certain disadvantages for social science research which are not always apparent to the casual reader of such statements, but which may be overcome by the null statement. A null hypothesis is more susceptible of objective proof as true or false than is a positively stated hypothesis, because the latter usually makes a normative assertion, and the null hypothesis substitutes for the normative term "improvement," the neutral terms "difference between scores," "changes in scores," and "difference between changes in scores." Now it is, of course, true that the magnitude of these scores is ordered to some initial value-judgment; high scores on such direct scales as those that measure social status, condition of the living room, or social participation, and low scores on the reverse scales that measure general adjustment and morale, similarly express desirable conditions or attitudes. Thus we cannot avoid value-judgments [17] upon the results of a social

IX Federal Reserve Bank shows a change from 94 for the first six months of 1939 to 97 for the corresponding period of 1940. The foregoing explanation is confirmed by a follow-up study in 1942 of 21 of the original 44 families still (1942) resident in the project. Visitors of the FPHA who made this study obtained scores on general adjustment and morale for 21 of the same housewives who had been interviewed in 1939 and in 1940, the other 23 families having moved out of the project since 1940. For these 21 women, the average general adjustment score changed 6.4 points, with a critical ratio of 2.39, or an indication of statistical significance at the 2-per-cent level! There was no statistically significant change in measured morale. Furthermore, the mean scores on social status of the 23 moved-out cases were higher than the 21 that remained, which suggests that when a period of adequate length is taken, public housing is then associated with an increase in general adjustment score despite the fact of differences in social status.

[17] There is a widely prevalent confusion in contemporary sociological theory which stems from semantic disorder. It is the idea that because the subject matter of socio-

program by merely substituting numerical expressions for the ordinary verbal expressions of the folk language. But this is not the point at issue. The significant thing is that the scales which yielded these scores were standardized for reliability and validity *previously* and *independently* of the value-problem now before us; the scores do not, therefore, represent judgments influenced by the immediate desires, compulsions, or needs of the moment for proving a case, and hence they possess elements of objectivity (verifiability) which are not present in value-judgments of the folk language. Let us now transform the single and positively stated hypothesis into a series of three null hypotheses and examine the factual evidence which supports them or which may lead us to reject them.

1. There are *no changes* in social participation, condition of the living room, and percentage use-crowded, if differences in composition of the experimental group and the control group are held constant [18] in respect to the 10 matching factors, race of husband, employment of husband, occupation of husband, number of persons in the family, income of family, race of wife, employment of wife, occupation of wife, age of wife, and years education of wife.

The evidence: Table 6 shows in rows 3 and 8 for all columns that *changes were obtained* as a result of the experiment. Hence the evidence fails to support, or conversely it disproves, the first null hypothesis.

2. The observed changes in social participation, condition of the living room, and percentage use-crowded are *not greater than* those

---

logical study is the value-motivated behavior of human beings it becomes impossible therefore to avoid normative considerations, and hence that sociological theory must remain a social philosophy and cannot be divorced from values. Such muddled thinking misses the essential points, which are these: while it is true that human relations, the subject matter of most sociological research, *are* largely ordered to normative considerations, it is nevertheless important and entirely possible *to keep value-judgments out of the authentic language of scientific method in sociological research.* These distinctions are clearly indicated in our argument for the advantages of the null hypothesis in studies of human relations. Although values are a proper and legitimate *subject of study,* they need not intrude into the methodological procedures of research to distort and to invalidate them. (See chap. vi, pp. 141–142, chap. vi, pp. 158–161, and chap. vii, pp. 176–181.)

[18] In the sense of control or regulation of extreme variations.

that could occur between two groups selected by random sampling from the same population.

The evidence: Table 6 shows in row 4 that all of these changes are statistically significant for the experimental group of residents, thus disproving the second null hypothesis in this respect. But for the control group of non-residents only column (1) of row 9 shows a

TABLE 6. Changes in Measures of Social Effects of Housing, 1939 to 1940

Groups Compared		Measures of Social Effect			
		Mean Social Participation Scores	Mean Scores on Condition of the Living Room	Percentage Use-crowded [a]	
		(1)	(2)	(3)	
Residents (N = 44)	1939	1.73	−0.20	50.00	1
	1940	6.34	+3.00	6.00	2
	Changes	+4.61	+3.20	−44.00	3
	Critical ratios	+3.69	+2.28	−4.44	4
	Multiple Critical Ratio		+6.01		5
Non-residents (N = 38)	1939	2.76	+3.50	44.70	6
	1940	4.87	+2.20	28.90	7
	Changes	+2.11	−1.30	−15.80	8
	Critical ratios	+2.88	−1.14	−1.43	9
	Multiple Critical Ratio		+1.82		10
Differences in Changes [b]		+4.50	+4.50	28.20	11
Critical Ratios		+1.90	+2.60	+4.11	12
Multiple Critical Ratio			+4.97		13

[a] In column (3) a negative sign (−) is interpreted as a gain, since it expressed a decline in percentage use-crowded.

[b] Changes in favor of residents, i.e., changes of residents in excess of gains of non-residents.

statistically significant difference. But when the multiple critical ratio is calculated it will be observed that for a pattern of response (combining all three measures of social effect), the *pattern of change,* row 5, is 6.01 in statistical significance for the experimental group of residents, whereas for the control group of non-residents in row 10 it is only 1.82, or not statistically significant. Thus the evidence of Table 6 disproves the second null hypothesis.

3. The observed differences between changes in social participation, condition of the living room, and percentage use-crowded are *not greater than* those that could occur frequently between two groups selected by random sampling from the same population.

The evidence: The differences in changes between the two groups are all substantial, as shown in row 11, but taken individually they are statistically significant only for measures on condition of the living room and percentage use-crowded, columns (2) and (3) of row 12. But again, when the *pattern of change* in response (combining all three measures) is taken as the criterion of significance, we note in row 13 that the multiple critical ratio is 4.97, or of high statistical significance. Thus this evidence disproves the third null hypothesis.

Where does this leave us? How can we state the net result? It leaves us with the conclusion that all three null hypotheses are not supported by the factual evidence, and this is not a process of setting up straw men to be knocked down. Our net conclusion is that the residents did change significantly in the social pattern of their response to a change in housing from slum living to a public housing project, whereas the control group of families which remained in the same slum dwellings throughout the experimental period of one year changed only to a degree which could occur so frequently as a fluctuation of random sampling as to be insignificant of any real change in their condition.

It will be observed that one of the conditions of the first null hypothesis is the constancy of the ten matching factors. These factors were held constant throughout the period of the experiment. A further word is relevant, however, as to the procedure in matching. The matching process when carried out in strict manner involves identical individual matching, that is, each individual in the experimental group is matched against another individual in the control group exactly similar in respect to the ten matching factors. Since this rigorous process of matching [19] inevitably leads to heavy eliminations of cases that cannot be paired on all factors, we resorted to the expedient of pairing two or more from the experimental group against one case of the control group within a stated range. To put the matter in different phraseology, the families in the non-resident group were paired against the families in the resident group when one or more non-resident families had the same classification according to the list of matching factors as one or more of the resident families. As indicated, this procedure was less rigorous than identical individual matching but gave us greater freedom in the pairing process, prevented excessive elimination of cases, yielded terminal groups of larger size, and was followed by determinate results.

Final proof that the gains of the residents are *due solely to their improved housing* would require that we had listed all the community and personal influences that operated in the period studied and then controlled, by matching, all of these differences *excepting only* the fact that the resident group were in the project and the non-resident group were in the slum. Obviously such a task would have been impossible to perform. We did, however, control by matching ten factors of a personal and social nature, which, if not controlled, might have explained the differences eventually found. With these ten factors [20] controlled or held constant throughout the experiment, we found by application of probability formulas that the differences measured could not have been due to chance in any reasonable expectation that reasonable persons would insist upon.

Sociological research continually reveals the existence of configurations and patterns of several factors. One such pattern of factors discovered in this study was the occurrence together of higher social participation score with improved condition of the living room and less use-crowding. Since we have hitherto been dealing

[19] The problem of interpreting differences or changes in the means of non-random samples, such as the experimental group and the control group of this housing study, is reserved for discussion in chap. VII.

[20] The reader is again reminded that there were really not 10 controls but 13 controls, since 3 were added as the study proceeded. See p. 68, footnote 14.

with these conditions in terms of scores (numerical symbols), it may be helpful to show the gross facts of observation from which these scores were derived. Tables 7, 8, 9, and 10 do this.

Table 7 shows that the residents gained at every level of participa-

TABLE 7.   Social Participation of Resident and Non-resident Groups

Social Participation Levels	Residents Frequency of Types of Participation		Non-residents Frequency of Types of Participation	
	1939	1940	1939	1940
None	29	16	26	13
1. Member	14	44	15	30
2. Attend	12	42	16	30
3. Contribute	13	37	13	24
4. Committee	0	5	1	2
5. Office	0	4	3	3
Total families	44	44	38	38

tion at least twice as much as the non-residents gained. The question now may be asked, What kind of organizations were included in these gains? Table 8 supplies the answer. It will be seen that the

TABLE 8.   Organizations Participated in by Resident and Non-resident Groups

Types of Social Organizations	Residents Number of Persons Participating			Non-residents Number of Persons Participating		
	1939 (1)	1940 (2)	Diff. (2–1)	1939 (1)	1940 (2)	Diff. (2–1)
1. Sumner Field Association	0	13	13	0	0	0
Mothers' Club	0	4	4	0	0	0
2. Neighborhood house clubs	1	1	0	0	1	1
3. Church or Sunday school clubs	7	11	4	16	17	1
	1	2	1	1	2	1
4. Unions	0	1	1	0	1	1
5. Other	6	14	8	7	12	5
Total	15	46	31	24	33	9

greatest gains of the residents were in (1) the Sumner Field Tenants' Association and its subsidiaries, (2) Sunday school, and (3) other organizations. What was the nature of these "other organizations"? Table 9 supplies the facts. It will be seen that in "other organiza-

TABLE 9.   Types of Social Organizations Included in the "Other" or Miscellaneous Classification in Table 8

Residents		Non-residents	
1939	1940	1939	1940
2 Social		2 Social	
2 Insurance		2 Veterans	2 Veterans
1 Bowling		1 Lodge	1 Lodge
1 Bridge	2 Bridge	1 Kindergarten	1 Mother's
	1 Mahjong	Mother's Club	1 Women's
	1 Home Ec.	1 Scout	1 Scout
	1 Delta Theta Pi		3 Card
	1 W.F.B.A.		(or Bridge)
	1 Sokol		
	3 P.T.A.		
	1 Charity		3 P.T.A.
	1 Relief Corps		
	1 Scout		
	1 Citizen's		
6	14	7	12

tions," the residents gained by diversification and variety in their social contacts, probably a beneficial gain.

An explanation of the scores on condition of the living room and the subsequent differences or gains in these scores that were summarized in Table 6 can be obtained by examining Part II of the *Social Status Scale*.[21] In spite of the apparent subjectivity of these

[21] The portion of the *Social Status Scale* referred to is as follows:

PART II: CONDITION OF ARTICLES IN LIVING ROOM

To provide some objective rating of qualitative attributes of the living room, such as "Aesthetic atmosphere" or "general impression," the following additional items may be noted. The visitor should check the words that seem to describe the situation. Some of the weights are of minus sign, and so operate as penalties to reduce the total score of the home.

categories of observation, they are in fact very reliable, as has been shown by coefficients of reliability of $+.72$ to $+.97$ obtained from repeated observations of the same homes.

Table 6, which measures differences and gains in terms of the percentage of families use-crowded, may be explained by the information contained in Table 10. Here it will be seen that the 22 families

TABLE 10. Changes in Use-crowding of Resident and Non-resident Groups

Type of Use-Crowding	Residents N = 44		Non-residents N = 38	
	1939	1940	1939	1940
1. Dining room..............	1	0	3	1
2. Kitchen...................	0	0	0	0
3. Bedroom, or DR & K......	21	3	14	9
4. BR & DR & K............	0	0	0	1
Total	22	3	17	11

(or 50 per cent of the 44 resident families) classified as use-crowded used their living room as a dining room also in one case in 1939 and had no such double use in 1940. They used their living room as a bedroom also, or as a dining room and kitchen also, in 21 cases in 1939. But in 1940 there were only three such cases. This was a real

18. Cleanliness of room and furnishings:
   a. Spotted or Stained (-4)_____
   b. Dusty (-2)_____
   c. Spotless and dustless $(+2)$_____
19. Orderliness of room and furnishings
   a. Articles strewn about in disorder (-2)_____
   b. Articles in place or in useable order $(+2)$_____
20. Condition of repair of articles and furnishings
   a. Broken, scratched, frayed, ripped, or torn (-4)_____
   b. Articles or furnishings patched up (-2)_____
   c. Articles or furnishings in good repair and well kept $(+2)$_____
21. Record your general impression of good taste
   a. Bizarre, clashing, inharmonious, or offensive (-4)_____
   b. Drab, monotonous, neutral, inoffensive (-2)_____
   c. Attractive in a positive way, harmonious, quiet and restful $(+2)$_____

gain in the functional purpose of the living room and represented less confusion of function in 1940 than in 1939. Similar analysis is shown for the non-resident group, which gained much less in these respects.

Table 8 shows for row 1, column (2), a gain in social participation for 17 persons in the experimental group of resident families and none for the control group. This result is clearly an end achieved by virtue of the social program of public housing. But notice that even when these 17 are eliminated from the comparison, the entries in rows 3 to 5, inclusive, for the residents still show a net gain over the control group in the number of participating individuals, that is, 14 as compared with 9. This result may perhaps be interpreted as an effect of the complex of housing factors operating as a cause.

The abiding purpose of the two experimental designs in which the time factor is a component, the projected experimental design and the ex post facto experimental design, is to discover a basis for generalization or for prediction. Ordinarily it would be sufficient to select random samples and to identify the probability model relevant to the kind of data manipulated to be able to generalize to a universe. But, as we shall see in Chapter VII, the ideal condition of randomization both to obtain the control of unknown influences and to achieve a reliable basis for generalization is denied us because of obstacles inherent in the usual social situation. Hence the only course to follow to attain this basis of generalization is to repeat [22] the

[22] A recent study of the social effects of public housing suffers from two defects: First, although it was made during 1942 and 1943, and is a before and after study, it did not utilize the available techniques and tools of measurement reported in the Minneapolis housing study described herein, although these results were published in December, 1940, and hence missed an opportunity to repeat an experimental design study on like subjects under like conditions; and second, it failed to avoid normative bias, a point commented upon by Bertram J. Black, who says of this Newark housing study that it is ". . . a curious mixture of analyses by social scientists and of a presentation for publicity purposes. Testimonials, opinion polls, and conclusions are slanted to meet the needs of the proponents for public housing and detract from the adequacy of the study as a scientific document . . . ," and again, "This reviewer hopes that when such analyses are made, the presentation of the findings be divorced completely from the desires of the housing authority for material to be used for publicity . . ." (pp. 91–92 in the *Journal of Housing,* June, 1945). The study here cited is that by Jay Rumney and Sara Shuman, *The Social Effects of Public Housing*

experiment under like conditions; if verification of results in several experiments ensues, we may calculate probabilities with some degree of assurance.

An Experimental Study of Staff Stimulation to Social Participation and Social Adjustment [23]

The extra-curricular activities of university students are a controversial problem in the opinion of many persons. It is claimed that such organizational activities on a university campus serve as an agency of social adjustment. Reuben Hill conducted a study at the University of Wisconsin from August, 1940, to June, 1942, to ascertain by projected experimental design whether the claim of advantages in student participation in extra-curricular activities did in fact make for better social adjustment. Among the students themselves there is a tendency to place higher value on such activities than upon classroom learning, and university counselors have frequently utilized social participation in their efforts to improve the personal adjustment of individual students.

The Wisconsin Union building provided a laboratory for the training of campus leaders, and the Division of Social Education, established to provide recreational services to students, was interested to discover the effect of its program of staff stimulation to participation in extra-curricular activities upon the scholastic achievement and the social adjustment of students. Thus it seemed advisable to try to find an answer to certain questions of policy and social action in this situation. Some eight previous studies of student extra-curricular activities tended to show the favorable effects of participation on both scholastic achievement and the social adjustments of college students.[24]

To bring this program to a test by experimental design of study,

in Newark, N. J., published by the Housing Authority of the City of Newark, November, 1944, and republished in March, 1946. This study illustrates the point that repetition of experimental study on similar subjects under like conditions with like methods is desirable if social research is to advance beyond an atomistic stage.

[23] "An Experimental Study of Social Adjustment," by Reuben Hill. _American Sociological Review_, October, 1944, pp. 481–494.

[24] _Ibid._, pp. 481–482.

the following working hypothesis was formulated: "Staff stimulation to participation in extracurricular activities results in improved scholastic achievement and improved social adjustment of college students." [25]

Since many factors combine to produce the effects of scholastic achievement and social adjustment, it was necessary at the outset to choose for control certain known factors which, if allowed to vary, might themselves produce the expected effect, quite apart from the program of staff stimulation by counseling, which latter was the causal factor to be measured. There were 15 factors selected for this control by matching on frequency distributions. These may be grouped as follows: three biological factors (age, sex, and health); one personality factor (rating by high school principal); three scholarship factors (American Council percentile rank, percentile rank in high school, and scholastic average the first semester in college); four social participation factors (church affiliation, fraternity affiliation, social participation in high school, and social participation as freshmen in the university); two social opportunity factors (size of home community and size of high school); and two social status factors (type of residence and degree of self-support).

The population or universe sampled consisted of 1306 freshman students in the College of Letters and Sciences in 1940. From an alphabetical listing of these students every other name was taken to form the experimental group; those remaining constituted the control group. Then the two groups were sorted out on one matching factor at a time. "Where differences in the distributions of the two groups occurred the offending individuals were noted and every *nth* card rejected until the distributions were equalized." [26] By this procedure fewer losses from matching were suffered and the samples remained representative. A total of 774 individuals was eliminated by inability to match them on the 15 control factors, leaving 266 each in the experimental group and the control group.

The next problem was the selection and administration of scales

[25] *Ibid.*, p. 483.
[26] *Ibid.*, p. 484.

to measure social adjustment before the experiment began and on the date of its termination. Conditions of reliability and validity [27] were met by two pencil-and-paper tests of social adjustment: J. P. Guilford's *Inventory of STDCR,* and J. J. Washburne's *Washburne Social Adjustment Inventory* (Thaspic edition). [28] The advantage of two inventories is that one served as a check upon the other. In November, 1940, these tests were administered in a series of meetings under the guise of gathering information for the junior dean's office. Two members of the staff of the Division of Social Education then began interviews of individuals in the experimental group. Care was taken to avoid reference to any specific questions in the tests. Individuals already active in student affairs were noted but given little counseling, the main effort at counseling being expended on the relatively inactive members of the experimental group. Key people in the student activity field, both faculty and student leaders, worked cooperatively with the counselors in directing individuals into student activities. When an individual expressed special interest in some field he was referred to the personnel head or student leader in that field. If undecided, a tentative program was worked out for him. In general, women students responded better than men students. In the 1941 guidance program the counselor used the student's record on the adjustment inventories for background information in interview. During this year 75 students dropped out of the experimental group and 78 from the control group, leaving continuous records on 86 in the experimental and 85 in the control when the experiment ended in June, 1942. It may be remembered that this period, especially early in 1942, was one of pressure to enter military service or wartime employment. In any event the numbers who dropped out were about equal in the two groups and in both some had left school, others failed to take the personality adjustment tests the second time or failed to return their questionnaires showing achievements in student activities. [29]

[27] See pp. 152–154.
[28] "An Experimental Study of Social Adjustment," *American Sociological Review,* October, 1944, p. 485.
[29] *Ibid.,* p. 488.

The results showed in a higher proportion of the experimental (treated) group active in student organizations and with its members participating in more activities per individual than was the case in the control group. About 400 student activities were evaluated and assigned weights so that the differences between the two groups showed up in higher mean score for the experimental group as well as in the number of responsible leadership positions held by its members.

In social adjustment measured by the Guilford *STDCR Inventory,* the experimental group students gained more in score than the controls in the depression factor (including feelings of unworthiness and guilt), the cycloid factor of strong emotional reactions and fluctuations in mood, in thinking introversion, and in Rhathymia (the happiness factor). Only in social introversion did the gain of the control group exceed the gain of the experimental group; and the average excess gain of the experimental group over the control, on the score for all factors, was 7.5 points, with a critical ratio of 1.74, not quite at the level of statistical significance.[30] For the Washburne test, the results were similar, but the differentials between gains in the two groups were somewhat smaller, with a critical ratio of 1.07.[31] Confirmation of the initial hypothesis that staff stimulation to participation in extra-curricular activities would result in improved social adjustment of college students is thus obtained by the results of these two tests; that is, the evidence supports and does not controvert the hypothesis. But since the critical ratios are small, the confirmation is not decisive.

On that part of the initial hypothesis which expected to find improvement in scholastic achievement, the results were indecisive, since the two groups remained practically constant throughout the experimental period.[32] This result is not surprising since there are good reasons to believe that no *group* improvement in scholarship occurs during the latter years of college because gains in mean scholarship score are more likely to be a result of selection (elimination of poorer students) than of the learning process. It needs to be remembered always that the earlier heavy elimination in the freshman year is a selective process. Since no improvement in scholastic

[30] *Ibid.,* p. 489.   [31] *Ibid.,* p. 490.   [32] *Ibid.,* p. 492.

achievement occurred, we may regard the scholastic record factor as another control, the sixteenth factor controlled in this study. Dr. Hill then revises his initial hypothesis to read:

"Staff stimulation to participation in extracurricular activities makes for improved social adjustment of college students but its effect on their scholastic achievement is negligible." [33]

Since this experiment in guided social participation was conducted with college students, it was possible to select the experimental group and the control group at random. That is to say, the group which received the benefit of staff stimulation to social participation did not have to be determined by need, as would have been the case in an experiment conducted in the natural community situation. For this reason an element of strength and integrity is added to the experiment which it seems difficult to attain under present circumstances with the pressure of the mores in social reform programs to relieve first the needy in the natural community. However, this comment should not be interpreted as an artificial limitation on this experiment which effectively disconnects it from the type of study reviewed in this book, and restricts application of the method used. As a matter of fact, student extra-curricular activities are extraordinarily varied and in many respects quite as free and voluntary as are the social activities in the natural community. Consequently it is the opinion of the author that Dr. Hill's use of randomization to equalize the unknown factors between the experimental and the control groups is an important illustration of what can be done, and should more often be done, in experimental studies in the natural community situation.

One final comment of a methodological nature may be worth making with respect to the hypothesis set up by Dr. Hill. Considering the advantages of the null hypothesis, stated on page 70, it may be of interest to consider the type of reformulation that would convert Dr. Hill's positive hypothesis into null hypotheses. The appropriate null hypotheses are:

1. There are *no changes* between two randomly selected groups of university sophomores in social participation, in scholarship, and in social adjustment after 18 months of avocational counseling of

[33] *Ibid.,* p. 493.

one group, when the initial differences in composition of the two groups with respect to 15 factors of biological nature, personality, social opportunity, scholarship, socio-economic status, and social activity are controlled by matching.

The evidence disproves this hypothesis with respect to social participation and social adjustment.

2. The observed differences between changes in social participation, scholarship, and social adjustment are *not greater than* would occur as the fluctuations of sampling between two groups drawn at random from the same population.

The evidence does not disprove this hypothesis with any degree of decisiveness, but it does tend to disprove it.

Stated as null hypotheses, the results are, of course, the same, the only advantage being that the evidence of facts becomes somewhat clearer as a test that supports or refutes the hypothesis.

DELINQUENCY TREATMENT IN THE CONTROLLED ACTIVITY GROUP [34]

Juvenile delinquency has become a concern of parents, teachers, and police in many communities. Successful treatment of this symptom of underlying social disorganization seldom occurs, and its prevention depends upon discovery of the causes and the eradication of these influences from the community. Dr. Shulman reports an experimental study of the effects on individual delinquents of a new method of social treatment by means of the controlled activity group. This method utilizes the techniques of group work in a novel manner and the purpose of his study was to test the results experimentally.

Clinical or sociological analysis was lacking in the earlier approaches of group work as a preventive of delinquency. Mass recreation and athletic competition did not succeed in curbing the problem because delinquents usually avoided supervised recreation or turned athletic competition into a new area for gang tactics. Even the supervised club met with only relative success. The development of projection methods of group therapy, consisting of loosely structured

[34] Harry M. Shulman, "Delinquency Treatment in the Controlled Activity Group," *American Sociological Review*, June, 1945, pp. 405–414.

groups, including trained adult leaders and neurotic children admitted individually, combined the characteristics of admission of the usual educational group with the democratic pattern of a friendship group. But even in this case the therapeutic group was a segregated one and was not applicable to a large number of children who were delinquents or potential delinquents.

The group guidance experiment reported by Dr. Shulman "conducted a new form of social group, the *controlled activity* group, set up within the structure of voluntary community recreation for normal children. Within the controlled activity group, problem and normal children mingled naturally in recreational activities." [35] The program was conducted under the auspices of the Social Research Laboratory of the City College of New York. It included a workshop and game-room program, classes in creative art, woodwork, metal and leather work, and met three sessions a week for two hours a session. Invited to this program were chronic truants, incorrigibles, serious personality problem children, and children charged with such serious offenses as arson and theft. Equal numbers of normal children were invited. Even the trained group leaders of the experiment were kept in ignorance of which were the delinquent children, and no school publicity was given to the experiment. An informal group structure was maintained and democratic and highly individualized relationships were maintained between children and student leaders. Such being the program, we now turn to the study of its empirical effects for three successive school semesters in three workshop centers for pupils from four public schools.

An experimental group of 155 children was selected to receive the controlled activity program, the results to be compared after three school semesters with a matched group of 155 children serving as the control group. The two groups consisted of boys $10\frac{1}{2}$ to $14\frac{1}{2}$ years of age, in grades 4A to 8A. Each group contained both normal children and problem children in the same proportions. The problem cases were obtained from official sources, and the non-problem

[35] *Ibid.*, p. 407. For a discussion of the six criteria for the establishment of a controlled activity group, the reader may consult Dr. Shulman's original article.

cases were obtained by serial selection from class roll-books of all children who had neither been reported by teachers or administrators as problems, nor ever dropped below B in conduct throughout their entire school histories. The schools from which the children came were in under-privileged and low-rent areas.

Each problem child in the experimental group was individually matched against a problem child in the control group; and each normal child in the experimental group was matched against another normal child in the control group. Six matching factors were chosen: age, sex, race (there were many Negro children), educational achievement, and general intelligence measured by the *Otis Classification Test,* and mechanical aptitude by the Stenquist paper-and-pencil test. There were 172 children eliminated as unable to match, and 8 more dropped out because of residence changes, leaving 130 for the experimental study. Among these, 74 were matched on all six control factors, 38 on five, 16 on four, and 2 on only three of the matching traits.

Striking differences were revealed by the tests between the problem children and the non-problem children. Table 11 shows these differences. Incidentally it should be noted that the problem children were equally divided, 25 in the experimental and 25 in the control group; likewise the non-problem children were 40 in each

TABLE 11.   Comparison of Problem Cases and Non-problem Cases [36]

Median Scores	All Problem Cases N = 50	All Non-problem Cases N = 80
	(1)	(2)
I.Q..............................	83	98
Educational quotient............	78	94
Mechanical aptitude percentile rating........................	17	31
Differences between groups......	Statistically significant on all measures	

[36] No tables appear in Dr. Shulman's original report. Those used here were constructed by the author from the statistical data in his text, since the tabular forms make his results clearer.

group. Thus each group consisted of mingled behavior types: individual children who had responded to the invitation to participate in the program and similar children constituting the control group.

The results of the program of controlled activity as a means of treating or of preventing juvenile delinquency will now be considered in the light of the test evidence derived from the projected experimental design. These results are expressed in measured differences in behavior in two contrasting types of social situations: (1) in the classroom situation and (2) in the community situation. Although the present book is concerned primarily with a description of experimental designs applied to the study of social programs in the community situation, it may be of interest to consider the evi-

TABLE 12.   Results of Experiment in Classroom Situation

Groups Compared	Per Cent Improved	Changes in Scores on Conduct Disorders [a]		
		Mild Items 1 to 5	Medium Items 6 to 10	Severe Items 11 to 15
	(1)	(2)	(3)	(4)
Problem cases of the experimental group [b]. N = 20	48	−6.2	+7.7	Improved
Problem cases of the control group........ N = 18	24	+8.5	−1.5	Grew worse
Differences......	24	14.7	9.2	Favor the experimental group
S.D. of this difference		9.13	7.0	

a On Haggerty-Wickman-Olson behavior rating scale.

(2) Items 1–5: disinterest, cheating, tardiness, lying, defiance.

(3) Items 6–10: over-activity, unpopularity with children, temper outbursts, bullying, speech difficulties.

(4) Items 11–15: imaginative lying, sex offenses, stealing, truancy, obscenity.

b Not all problem cases were available for case study.

dence of changes in behavior in the classroom situation shown in Table 12.

It will be observed that the improvement among problem children in the control group was only one-half the improvement of children in the experimental group which received the controlled activity program. This appears in column (1). Turning to the last column, (4), it will be noted that children in the treated group showed a decrease in the type of symptoms which characterize the matured delinquent personality, namely, in sex offenses, stealing, truancy, etc., and that the symptoms of the control group problem children worsened. The fact that column (3) shows an increase in conduct disorders among the problem children of the experimental group, and a decrease among problem children of the control group, is indicative of an increased emotional release arising from the emotional disturbance produced by experience in the workshops.

Probably more significant for social policy and social action are the results found in the community situation of the family and

TABLE 13.   Changes in Behavior in the Community Situation among Problem Cases

Periods of the Experiment	Changes in Family and Play Group Situations [a]			
	Experimental Group Problem Cases N = 20		Control Group Problem Cases N = 18	
	Medians	Range	Medians	Range
	(1)	(2)	(3)	(4)
After treatment..	43.5	33–55	40.5	24–50
Before treatment	37.0	27–45	39.5	29–49
Changes........	72% gained 2–17 point range of gain 9.5 mean point gain		33% gained 1–9 point range of gain 3.5 mean point gain	
	28% loss 2 mean point loss		66% loss 2 mean point loss	

[a] Based study of 13 of the 66 Baker-Traphagen items selected as a measure of behavior status.

play group for the problem children who received the treatment; certainly the test of these results by experimental study is of central interest in the theme of this book. Table 13 shows quite conclusively that the problem cases contained in the experimental group gained far more and lost far less than did the problem children in the control group which received no treatment. It is unfortunate that only 20 of the 25 problem cases of the experimental group could be followed in case study, and that only 18 of the 25 problem cases in the control group could be similarly followed up. However, the results do stand in striking contrast for the cases studied, despite the fact that 24 per cent of the original 50 problem children cases were lost.[37]

It is interesting to note that in this experimental study of the effects of social treatment, the measured gains were in several items highly significant in statistical meaning, whereas in the previous study of social adjustment reported by Dr. Hill the measured gains did not attain statistical significance despite the fact that they occurred in the expected direction. This does not mean, however, that the Shulman treatment was more successful than the Hill program. The Shulman program concerned cases of serious maladjustment; the Hill study was based on college sophomores, already a highly selected group in the direction of good adjustment. Thus we would expect significant gains in the former and be satisfied with much smaller gains in the latter, both results being indicative of the success of the program of social treatment respective to the quite different behavior standards of the subjects.

In consideration of the data presented, Dr. Shulman says, "We may conclude this analysis of experimental findings by stating that the results were positive both in the school class-room and in the family setting for the treated group, that the treatment program appeared to release tensions and aggressions, to replace delinquent patterns by patterns of emotional instability, and to modify per-

[37] The results of the Shulman experiment stand by themselves as true only for the number of cases studied, since the original groups of 155 each, and the terminal groups of 65 each, were selective samples of those who responded to the invitation to join the controlled activity group, in contrast to the Hill experiment in which randomization was the basis of selection, thus providing a basis for generalization to the population of all sophomores.

sonality disorders. The control problem group, by contrast, remained relatively static in school and in the family setting, some children improving slightly and the majority growing slightly worse in conduct." [38] These conclusions appear to be supported by the evidence, although without repetition of the experiment, under like conditions with similar subjects and like results, no generalization about the success of this type of treatment to juvenile delinquents in general can be made.

There remains to be considered the possible effect of factors not controlled by matching or of unknown factors. To guard the results against the intrusion of "concomitant beneficent variations in societal experience," [39] a study was made of the influence of the social backgrounds of both experimental and control problem groups, both before and after treatment, which if neglected might themselves explain the beneficial changes in behavior, rather than accepting the evidence of the results as due to treatment alone. In Table 14 are shown the changes in social background factors of family disorganization, defective social relationships, and improper discipline.

Comparison of columns (1) and (4), (2) and (5), (3) and (6) shows the existence of very marked similarities in the extent of social pathology and defective family relationships in family life of the surrounding community. As Shulman states it, "These facts lead to the conclusion that no measurable influences in the social environment of the two groups account for the marked improvement of the majority of the experimental group and the continued and slightly deteriorating misconduct of the majority of the control group of intensively studied cases." [40] Thus the conclusions about the effect of social treatment are strengthened, since Table 14 indicates that both groups were influenced in about equal degree by environmental influences that stemmed from the surrounding community life.

[38] Shulman, *op. cit.,* p. 413.

[39] It will be noted that these variations correspond to our own concept of natural recuperative social processes inherent in the community. See p. 92 below.

[40] Shulman, *op. cit.,* p. 414.

TABLE 14. Constancy of Background Factors in the Community

Characteristics and Trends of Family Background during the Period of Experiment	Community Background Factors					
	Experimental Group of Problem Cases N = 20 [a]			Control Group of Problem Cases N = 18 [a]		
	Family Disorganization	Defective Social Relationships	Improper Discipline	Family Disorganization	Defective Social Relationships	Improper Discipline
	(1)	(2)	(3)	(4)	(5)	(6)
1. Cumulative percentage.....	350	165	145	357	187	137
2. Combined factors.........	660			681		
3. Trend in family pathology......	40			38.5		
4. Improvement [b]	40			27.5		

[a] Not all problem cases were available for case study.

(1) and (4): percentage totals for items of broken homes, marital disharmony, public assistance, economic maladjustments, chronic illness, mental disease and deficiency, unethical or anti-social example in the home or neighborhood.

(2) and (5): percentage totals for items of evidences of defective social relationships such as: defective parental relationships, defective relationships to problem child, other defective relationships in the home, and defective community relationships.

(3) and (6): percentage totals for severe discipline or lax discipline.

[b] Commenting on the category of improvement during the experimental period, Shulman states on pp. 413–414, "How much an improvement in family social relationships between problem child and parents is itself a cause or a product of behavior improvement, is however, unclear. Twice as many instances occurred in the experimental as in the control group and contributed largely to the percentage difference."

A final comment may be made to point up a striking agreement in results that emerges from the Minneapolis housing study, the Wisconsin counseling study, and the New York study of the effects of treatment upon juvenile delinquency. It is this: in all these experimental studies the factor of participation in social activities was an important element. In the Wisconsin and New York studies this factor of social participation in group activities was associated with definitive gains or improvement in social adjustment as measured by standardized scales; and in the Minneapolis study increased social participation was associated with such other evidences of improvement in social adjustment as gains in score on condition of the living room and a decline in use-crowding.

These facts support a hypothesis previously stated by the author, namely, that there exist in the natural community social forces making for personal adjustment, and that these forces operate through and by way of social participation in the groups, clubs, and organizations of the natural community. We have called these forces natural recuperative social processes[41] which, if allowed free play, tend to build up and integrate the human personality, and operate like the processes of nature, without human design expressed in narrow means-ends schema. Physicians have long ago recognized the existence of natural recuperative processes in the human organism, and have come to rely upon hygiene, exercise, and rest as factors which may release these biological processes that re-create the organism. Likewise it seems entirely possible that in social treatment by social case work and social action programs, both consciously directed activities, perhaps too consciously directed, we have neglected to allow for the natural recuperative social processes that exist in the surrounding community. Certainly the evidence of these three experimental studies calls attention to the fact that the control group of families in the slum in Minneapolis gained in social participation during the period of the experiment, that the untreated students in the control group of the Wisconsin study also gained during the experimental period, and finally, that the gains of the control group of problem cases in the New York study were also of measurable degree. Thus it appears that disadvantaged groups of the community may experience gains without benefit of formal social treatment as this appears in case work and in social reform programs. If this hypothesis in verified in other studies it has im-

[41] F. Stuart Chapin, "Social Participation and Social Intelligence," *American Sociological Review*, April, 1939, pp. 157–166, especially p. 162.

plications of a very significant nature for all social treatment directed to the achievement of human adjustment.

All of these experimental studies stress the evidence of gains or improvement in individual adjustment of human beings. As we pointed out on pages 70–71 in our discussion of the advantages of the null hypothesis over the positively stated hypothesis, there is an element of risk in the use of value-terms such as "gain" and "improvement," since our natural desire is to demonstrate by the test of experimental study that a program of treatment has in fact (rather than in mere opinion) achieved its purpose. To avoid the bias of desire we suggested that the criterion of success of treatment be stated in terms of changes in measured traits, but that this substitution of numerical expression for the ordinary terms of the folk language did not eliminate the factor of value. The important point in this matter is that the scales used to measure the changes assumed to be induced by treatment were scales that had been standardized for reliability and validity *prior to* the beginning of the particular experimental test in which they were used. Thus, although the magnitude of scores expresses a value, this value was previously and independently determined so that it could not bias interpretation of results. It will be noted that in all four experiments described in this chapter the measures of adjustment were scales previously and independently standardized, and this fact lends to the results an element of objectivity and integrity that is highly important in the study of human relations.

It cannot be too emphatically stated that, in the study of problems of human relations to determine by experimental design the results of social treatment or social action, desire is ever present to warp interpretation. It is natural for the human student of human relations to find what he wishes to find. For this reason it is important to avoid an appraisal of results which relies upon opinion. The evidence of facts and, wherever possible, the evidence of measurement are more objective and convincing forms of confirmation. Consequently reliance upon opinion should be confined to the early stages of an experimental study, when decision is made upon which tools of observation or measurement are to be selected to provide criteria of effect; [42] and also to the definition of the ends or objectives or the effects to result. After this stage of the study has been passed, the evidence of facts and measurements should be allowed to fall where it may, and inference should flow freely from this evidence without regard to opinion.

[42] Lundberg makes a similar point when he says, "The only value judgments which any properly trained scientist makes about his data are judgments regarding their relevance to his problem." *Harper's Magazine,* December, 1945, p. 530.

Chapter V

EX POST FACTO EXPERIMENTAL DESIGN:
FROM PRESENT TO PAST

APPLICATIONS of the projected experimental design described in Chapter IV were made to trace and clarify our understanding of how some present causal complex of factors may produce an effect at a future date (see Table 2, Chapter II, page 32). Now our approach to the cause-and-effect relationship is made in reverse. In this chapter, therefore, we begin our study with a description of the *present situation as an effect* of some previously acting causal factors and attempt to trace back over an interval of time to some assumed causal complex of factors which began operating at an earlier date. This type of experimental study we have called the ex post facto experimental design.[1] Since Ernest Greenwood[2] has analyzed and described the logic of this design, we shall confine our attention to three examples: (1) the relationship of public housing in New Haven to juvenile delinquency; (2) the effects of length of high school education on economic adjustment in St. Paul; and (3) our recent and until now unpublished study of the relationship of factors expressed in rentals to the tuberculosis death rate in New York City.[3]

Two variations in the method of ex post facto experimental design will be described: (a) in which self-comparison of the *same individuals and families* is made at a present date and at some past date (the New Haven and St. Paul studies); and (b) in which comparison is made of populations in the *same areas* at a present date and some past date (the New York City study).

[1] Our first use of the concept, ex post facto experimental design, was made on p. 29 of *Research Memorandum on Social Work in the Depression,* by F. Stuart Chapin and Stuart A. Queen, Bulletin 39, Social Science Research Council, 1937.

[2] Ernest Greenwood, *Experimental Sociology: a Study in Method,* King's Crown Press, 1945, *passim.*

[3] We were assisted by Toimi E. Kyllonen, John N. Burrus, and Marvin J. Taves.

The first type of comparison is more accurate than the second and hence preferable whenever possible, since in the second type of comparison we may not be able to account for the influence of mobility expressed as in-migration or out-migration and we are obliged to rely upon a somewhat doubtful assumption of similarity or constancy of populations and their environments at the two dates. Then there is another limitation inherent in the ex post facto experimental design which applies to both variations. This is due to the restriction imposed upon us by the facts that *exist in the records* available to supply the data to be used. When an experimental test is made of the results of some social program of treatment or social action by the projected design in contrast to the ex post facto design, a record of all relevant facts or opinions, as the study may require, is obtained by interview, as we have described these operations in Chapter IV. In short, *we obtain* any information that may be required by interview, questionnaire, or schedule. Usually the information so obtained is essentially new data hitherto not written into any official or public record of a government census, an annual report, a formal document, or a health registration. Such is the case with respect to social attitudes or behavior expressed as morale or social adjustment; as social participation in memberships, attendance, committee assignments, and official positions in formally organized groups; as well as in other qualities too numerous to repeat at this point.

In ex post facto experimental design we are limited in choice of causal factors and in the selection of control factors to the information that exists in accessible records of the past behavior of the subjects studied. This is a serious limitation, but, despite this restriction on freedom of method and technique, there is in fact, as we shall see, a surprising number of available data for use.

Delinquency before and after Admission to a New Haven Housing Development [4]

It has often been claimed that good housing will diminish juvenile delinquency among children of slum families simply because evidence exists which shows the association of room-crowding, residence in deteriorated dwellings, and other housing deprivations with high rates of juvenile delinquency. But this evidence does not in itself alone prove that poor housing is a cause per se of juvenile delinquency. The first study in which any measure of success was realized to show a cause-and-effect rather than a mere associational relationship between poor housing and juvenile delinquency was made by Miss Naomi Barer in New Haven in 1944, and reported in 1945.

The years 1940 to 1944 were taken as the date of departure in a study of 317 families who had lived in one of the developments of the New Haven Housing Authority for periods varying from two and one-half to four and one-half years. The earlier records of these 317 families were then traced back over the period 1924 to 1940 before they had became residents of the public housing project. Then the records for the two periods were compared for incidence of juvenile delinquency.

There were 649 children in these families and about 70 per cent of the families were Negroes. During project occupancy the ages of the children were between 7 and 17 years. Records of the Juvenile Court were checked back to 1924 by the names of these children, together with their older brothers and sisters. The data for each year from 1924 to 1940 were then compared with the juvenile delinquencies recorded for these children to obtain incidence rates. Table 15 shows the results for the 17 years before entrance to the project compared with the four years of residence in the housing development.

The difference in rates shown in column (3) between 3.18 for the pre-public housing period and 1.64 for the residence period is approximately three times the significant difference (0.52), and hence may be regarded as statistically significant. One might conclude from these results that the chief difference in family living between

[4] Naomi Barer, "Delinquency Before, After Admission to New Haven Housing Development," *Journal of Housing,* December, 1945–January, 1946, based upon "The Effects of Improved Housing on Health," M.A. thesis in the Department of Public Health, Yale School of Medicine, 1945.

TABLE 15. Comparison of Recent Juvenile Delinquency Rates among Residents of the Housing Project with the Rates of the Same Group before Residence

Years	Total Number Child-Years in Families	Total Number Juvenile Delinquencies	Rate of Juvenile Delinquencies per 100 Children per Year
	(1)	(2)	(3)
1924–1940.....	1952	62	3.18
1940–1944.....	1401	23	1.64

the two periods, namely, residence in the public housing project, was the cause of the decline in juvenile delinquency rates.

But what of other factors? The author is careful at this point to inquire into the evidence of other factors. If the court record procedure had changed during the period, or if a notable.general decrease in juvenile delinquency had occurred since 1940, the results would have no significance. Changes in the conditions of the experiment of this sort did not apparently occur, for there was an *increase* of 9.1 per cent in total juvenile delinquency in New Haven for the years 1940 to 1941, as compared with the period 1927 to 1940. Thus the decline in juvenile delinquencies among the project family children took place within the larger community in which a substantial increase in the juvenile delinquency rate was recorded.

Doubtless the reader will think of other factors that require study before the results of this experimental test of housing and juvenile delinquency can be taken as a basis for generalization about the effects of good housing. But the results seem to establish a strong presumption that the factor of improved housing played an important rôle and to this extent support the hypothesis that good housing may cause a decline in juvenile delinquency rather than merely be associated with a decline. Obviously this promising experimental test of an important relationship needs to be repeated. The simplicity of the method commends it for wider application. If replication with like methods upon similar subjects under similar conditions yields results that confirm these findings, we shall have taken a real step forward in our understanding of some of the factors causally associated with juvenile delinquency.

THE EFFECTS OF LENGTH OF HIGH SCHOOL EDUCATION ON ECONOMIC ADJUSTMENT IN THE COMMUNITY OF ST. PAUL[5]

The working hypothesis of this study was: A greater degree of progress in high school leads to a correspondingly higher degree of economic adjustment in the community. Thus, the two variable factors whose relationship is to be measured are ones that lie at the heart of educational policy. Do we not spend millions of dollars annually to support high school education on the assumption that this hypothesis is a true statement of social relationship? Of course there are other purposes of high school education besides economic adjustment, but certainly economic adjustment is one of the most practical considerations.

This experiment was based upon the high school records and community experiences of 2127 boys and girls who left four St. Paul high schools in the school year of 1926, as graduates or after having completed from one to three years of their high school course. There were only four St. Paul high schools at this date *so that the experiment concerns the whole universe and not a sample.* The year 1926 was taken because it was the earliest year for which comparable records on a large number of students were available. Moreover, since the follow-up was to the year 1935, there was thus a period of nine years in which these individuals could work out economic adjustments.

Having set up the working hypothesis of the experiment, it next becomes necessary to secure measures of the two variables to be observed. The independent variable, school progress, was measured

[5] Appeared originally as part of "Design for Social Experiments," *American Sociological Review,* December, 1938. The experiment is that of Mrs. Helen F. Christiansen, "The Relation of School Progress, Measured in Terms of the Total Amount of School Attendance or Course Completion, to Subsequent Economic Adjustment," M.A. thesis, University of Minnesota Library, June, 1938.

by the number of years of the high school course completed when the student left school in 1926. Of the total of 2127 boys and girls, 1130 graduated from high school in 1926 after completing four years and 997 dropped out in 1926 after having been in high school for the regular one or two or three years of the course. The measure of economic adjustment selected for the dependent variable was the percentage of shifts on jobs from 1926 to 1935 that involved no change in salary or an increase in salary as contrasted to the percentage of shifts that involved decrease in salary.

Now it is perfectly obvious that these are extremely crude measures. Factors of age difference as between those who left at the end of the freshman high school year and those who remained to graduate might affect economic adjustment. Sex differences are often significant. Boys or girls from homes of higher status would have an advantage in gaining and holding employment not possessed by children from homes of lower status. Differences in the nationality of the parents would influence the chances of getting a job. The neighborhood of the home from which the boy or girl came might be a factor in economic adjustment. The intelligence or mental ability of the different individuals would exert its influence upon securing a job, holding the job, and upon promotion in rank and salary on the job. This network of factors is also one of interrelationship. An American boy whose father was a successful professional man living in a restricted neighborhood would have several factors combined in his favor in comparison with the Jewish boy whose father was a clerk and lived in a deteriorated neighborhood. Since every one of these variable factors is recognized by sensible people as influencing the course of individual economic progress, the way to obviate their disturbing influence is to control them. Here, therefore, we come again to our crucial problem of controls.

In the Christiansen study each of these six factors, chronological age, sex, nationality of parents, father's occupation, neighborhood status, and mental ability (by computing high school marks because the measurement by I.Q. was not available) was controlled. The chief contribution of the study was to demonstrate the comparative

value of different methods of controlling these factors. The pragmatic test of the value of different methods of control is the effect
upon the closeness of relationship between the measured change in
the dependent variable and the measured change in the independent
variable. But before we can present the results of this comparison it is
necessary to describe some of the practical procedures that inter-
vene between the formulation of the working hypothesis and the
measurement of the results of observation under conditions of
control.

It took a full year of systematic work in home visits and interviewing to trace the 1130 graduates of 1926, and the 997 drop-outs of
1926, to their status of 1935. In this process, there was a shrinkage of
933 individuals in the total. Of the number lost, 21 were deceased,
42 had moved out of town, 575 could not be traced in the follow-up,
and 295 had records so incomplete as to make comparison worthless.
Thus, of the original 2127, there were located a group of 671 graduates and a group of 523 drop-outs.[6] See Figure 5, flow chart.

Christiansen thus had a control group of 523 drop-outs and an
experimental group of 671 graduates. It was then necessary to control the six factors mentioned as potential disturbing influences on
the real relationship of high school education to economic adjustment in after life. The process of gaining control began with the
matching of a child from the control group and another child from
the experimental group for sex and nationality of parents. This reduced the two groups to smaller groups with identical proportions
in sex division and in the distribution of parental nationality. At
this point the control of factors by identity through individual
matching had to be supplanted by control through the correspondence of frequency distributions on each factor. The reason for this
change was that the condition of individual identity on a factor by
matching eliminated so many cases that the sample dwindled in size
at an alarming rate after each new control was set.

The correspondence of frequency distributions on a given variable
factor is a far less rigorous control of this variable factor than is

[6] *Ibid.*, p. 7.

identity by matching individual with individual, but it is probably the most frequently used method of control in contemporary experimental studies. Its selection and application on grounds of reducing the attenuation of the sample is justified when the results of

FIGURE 5.   Flow Chart

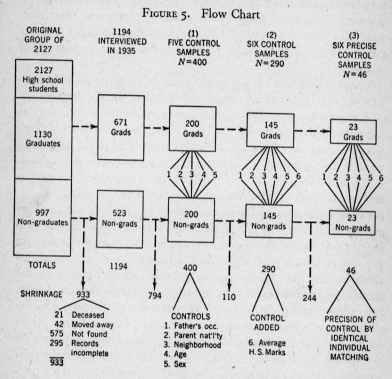

the experiment are significant. When the results are not significant and no other explanation is reasonable, then it is necessary to resort to the more expensive process of individual matching, but this means repetition of the experiment, or at least increasing the number of cases observed.

Setting the six controls reduced the final sample to a total of only 290 cases, 145 in the control group and 145 in the experimental group, a decline of 86.4 per cent from the original group of 2127 students! This is the price of observation under conditions of control. The longer the list of controls and the more rigorous their method of application, the smaller the final sample. At this point, some statisticians may say that we end up with a sample too small to be representative of conditions in a large original group, but let me remind them that an experiment is designed to obtain a homogeneous and "pure" sample. In fact, our sample has been purged of the very factors that made for heterogeneity in the original group and whose presence obscured the real relationship between the factors we set out to study. To discover the *real* relationship between a magnet and iron, we must have "pure" iron and not iron ore that is complicated by the presence of other minerals and metals, which it would be if "representative" of the original ore. Homogeneity, not representativeness, is *the* essential condition to the discovery by a single experiment of a real relationship between two factors. Consequently, if the present experiment shows that there *is* a relationship between the amount of high school education and the degree of subsequent economic adjustment, this relationship is more likely to be a *real* one than is the case under conditions in which the social situation is complicated by several uncontrolled factors. Within certain limits (the limits of the given experiment), the homogeneity of the two sub-samples is more important than their representativeness of variable factors that originally obscured the relationship.[7]

Finally, if we turn now to the differences in economic adjustment of the control group of drop-out students and the experimental group of graduates we find that 88.7 per cent of the graduates experienced no changes in salary or had increases in salary from 1926 to 1935, whereas 83.4 per cent of the drop-outs reported increases or no changes in salary from 1926 to 1935. Putting it the other way, only 11.3 per cent of the graduates suffered salary decreases in this period, whereas 16.6 per cent of the drop-outs suffered salary decreases. This is a small difference of 5.3 per cent.

When the length of high school education before drop-out is

[7] This is the case because random samples are seldom an available medium for social treatment in the free community situation as was shown in chap. IV in the discussion of the Minneapolis housing study. This will also be considered in chap. VII.

analyzed,[8] we find that 74.1 per cent who left school in 1926 at the end of one year of high school had salary increases or no changes in salary during the period 1926–1935; and of those who ended two years of high school, 85.1 per cent were adjusted economically; and 89.6 per cent of those who ended three years of high school were adjusted. Thus, in general, the longer the period of high school education, the higher the percentage of adjustment in the economic terms used as a criterion. None of these differences are statistically significant as single differences. The important point is that they are consistent and in the same direction. It is a matter of opinion whether small differences that are corroboratory and in the same direction are as important as differences that are large and statistically significant. Our opinion is unequivocally that small differences in the same direction may be as important as one large difference that is statistically significant. There are two reasons for this opinion. First, social phenomena are complex and not likely to show large differences because of the configurational character of the social situation. The separate factors in a social situation are usually functionally related. Second, the conventional tests of the significance of sampling are based upon the theory of random samples, and in the present stage of experimental work, as we have attempted to show, it is the terminal homogeneity and purity in the sample, rather than initial representativeness of heterogeneity, that is important in demonstrating the *real* relationship between two variable factors.

The Christiansen experiment involved the collection of other information than that about salary changes, and the analysis of this information revealed the existence of other small differences in favor of the experimental group of graduates. For example, it was found that the percentage of non-graduates or drop-outs who reported non-voting was 24 per cent as compared with the non-voting graduates, which were 14.5 per cent of the total.[9] It was found that the average number of interests in activities tended to increase with the number of years' high school education: one-year individuals, .50; two-year individuals, .67; three-year individuals, .63, and graduates, .91.[10] Likewise, the average number of years' additional education in-

[8] Christiansen, *op. cit.,* pp. 64, 89.   [9] *Ibid.,* p. 38.   [10] *Ibid.,* p. 41.

creased with the amount of high school education.[11] One-year individuals had an average of .46 years, two-year individuals, .73 years, three-year individuals, .89 years, and graduates, 1.45 years. It will be observed that all of these differences are small but that they are predominantly in the same direction, that is, they show more favorable adjustment in direct proportion to the amount of high school education. One last measure of economic adjustment was found in the occupational class to which these young people had climbed by 1935. This rough measure of economic adjustment was also distinctly favorable to the graduate group, which had four times as many individuals in the highest occupational class as the nongraduate group. Contrariwise, the graduate group had smaller numbers in the lower occupational classes.[12]

Thus the Christiansen experiment, in spite of the crudity of measuring devices used, was nevertheless successful if the argument in favor of corroboratory small differences is accepted,[13] because these small differences—in salary changes, percentage voting, average number of interests in activities, average number of additional years' education, and occupational class attained—all support the hypothesis by showing evidence of better adjustment with every increase in the amount of high school education. Doubtless there will be those who will observe that the experiment has merely proved that which we expected to be true. But justification by expectation and wishful thinking is quite a different thing from corroboration by factual evidence. On the other hand, there may be critical persons who will observe that the results of this experiment are almost too good to be true. To all such, we may reply that the evidence is available for critical appraisal in the thesis, and that in any event we do not claim that one successful experiment proves a relationship to be true. The experiment must be repeated and the results verified

[11] *Ibid.*, p. 47.
[12] *Ibid.*, pp. 50, 58.
[13] It will be remembered that the pattern of small differences as evidence supporting the result of experimental design was summarized by the device of the multiple critical ratio in the Minneapolis housing study of chap. iv. It was not used in the St. Paul study because of the crude character of the original observations in this study.

before the *principle* is established on factual evidence rather than on wishful opinion.

In this experiment, we have found that control of such variable factors as age, sex, nationality of parents, occupation of father, neighborhood status, and high school marks is sufficiently adequate control of the social situation to lead to definite scientific results. What would have happened if we had exercised a more rigorous control by the device of identity secured through individual pairing for every variable factor instead of relying on the rough control of correspondence between distributions in the case of the four factors of age, father's occupation, neighborhood status, and high school marks?

The answer to this question was obtained by actually pairing against each individual in the control group of drop-outs another individual from the experimental group of graduates of the same sex, identical chronological age, the same parental nationality, the same father's occupation, the same neighborhood status, and identical high school marks. This process of more exact control reduced the total from 290 to only 46, of which 23 were in the control group of drop-outs and 23 were in the experimental group of graduates. When the economic adjustment of these two contrasting groups is examined, the following results emerge: 92 per cent of the experimental group of graduates had salary increases or no change in salary from 1926 to 1935, whereas only 58 per cent of the control group of drop-outs experienced salary increases or no salary change for the period. This is a difference of 34 per cent in favor of the graduates. In comparison, the difference was only 5.3 per cent for sub-groups of the 290 cases under less rigorous controls. Thus, the labor of more exact control was amply repaid because it demonstrated, in a more decisive manner and in terms of a difference statistically significant, the superior economic adjustment of the experimental group of graduates. In this case, the real relationship was more clearly demonstrated by more rigorous controls. Of course, this further analysis might have disclosed that the real relationship was less marked, rather than more marked. Scientifically speaking, the use of controls aids us in getting at the underlying true relationship, *whatever* that relationship may be. Whether the analysis confirms the hypothesis or disproves it is a consideration entirely irrelevant to the experimental method.

We may now summarize the conclusions from our analysis of the Christiansen experiment. (1) If there is a real relationship between two social variables and it is a substantial one, then even crude controls of other variable factors will demonstrate the existence of this relationship. (2) Demonstration of the real relationship between two observed variables may be established within the limits of one experiment quite as decisively by many small differences that are in the same direction and are in agreement as by the conventional criterion of statistically significant differences. (3) When the number of cases observed is large, it repays the effort to apply control of variable factors by the method of identity through individual matching, since this procedure will demonstrate with finality (within the limitations of the given experiment) the degree of real relationship by satisfying the criterion of a statistically significant difference. To illustrate this latter point, we find that a difference of 5.3 per cent after crude control has a critical ratio of only 1.24, whereas the difference of 34.0 per cent after more rigorous control has a critical ratio of 2.90. Since such a difference would occur by chance only once in 267 (or 3.74 times in 1000) random cases, we conclude the difference is statistically significant of a real difference.[14] Furthermore, since the critical ratio of 2.90 is computed from a difference between extremely pure samples, its significance is much enhanced by this fact. The reason is that the use of the standard error of a difference as a device to determine significance is based on the theory of sampling that derives directly from chance in the throwing of identical coins. In most research, such a degree of homogeneity as found in identity is usually lacking, hence the very exacting rule of three times the standard error or one case in 370 is adopted as a guard against fluctuations caused by great heterogeneity. When, however, as in the case of the Christiansen experiment, we obtain a high degree of homogeneity by selection and control, then a critical

[14] H. E. Garrett, *Statistics in Psychology and Education*, 1930 ed., p. 134, and G. U. Yule, *An Introduction to the Theory of Statistics*, 1912 ed., p. 310.

ratio of 2.0 may be accepted as quite significant of a real difference. The Christiansen experiment is an ex post facto experiment and began with conditions of adjustment as they existed in 1935 and then by the method of control traced the relationship back to conditions that existed at the beginning, that is, in 1926. Wherever adequate records are available the ex post facto experiment is possible. Hence, it is very important to have good records of relevant factors to a relationship among variables that we wish to test.

We have stated our opinion that the controls in the Christiansen experiment were crude in spite of its obvious success. Let us elaborate the reasons why these controls were crude. Pairing on the factor of chronological age, for example, usually assumes that this device gives control of the degree of maturity of two individuals, and yet it is common knowledge that two persons of the same sex who are both 18 years of age may not be equally mature. Within the sex factor there are doubtless differences in sex appeal which may have some marginal influence upon course grades given by a teacher of the opposite sex. In the case of such rough social status measures as nationality of parents, father's occupation, and neighborhood rating, there would be slight differences in spite of identical pairing. What then is the explanation of the successful effect of such unprecise pairing? The explanation probably lies in the fact that the separate status factors tend to supplement rather than to offset one another. Similarly, there is probably a cumulative weighting of the factor of mental ability through a combination and reinforcement of influences inherent in father's occupation and high school grades. The higher the father's occupation, the higher the increment of mental ability, even if slight, and this supplements the slightly higher mental ability that usually goes with higher marks in high school studies. In fact, there is some support for this explanation in the results of statistical analysis of social status in which a correlation matrix of five factors of status, income, education, occupation, participation, and social status score resulted in an approach to zero for the conventional tetrad equations.

Also, a recent factor analysis of the same correlation matrix by Louis Guttman of the University of Minnesota, using a more elaborate method, clearly demonstrated the existence of a "pure" status factor as a general factor.[15] The factors other than status may also have underlying factors in common. If so, then we have an explanation of the surprisingly decisive result of using the technique of identical pairing on essentially unmeasured factors. If further research with the experimental method should support this explanation, then the problem of controls is greatly simplified whenever we have reason to believe that separately rated or separately measured factors possess a common general factor. In fact, such an explanation would supply the justification empirically, at least, for a systematic search for control factors that had a general factor in common. It would then be unnecessary to devise elaborate and expensive scales of measurement because, if the factors chosen for control were influential, they would not need to be precisely measured provided they possessed a general factor in common. Of course the requirement of more precise methods still obtains. Our conclusion merely applies to the present rough techniques of the experimental method used in empirical studies.

Review of Control by Matching for Precision of Control [16]

Many studies of social relationships qualify their conclusions by the statement: "Other things being equal," so and so takes place. For example, we attempt by public education to equalize opportunity. But how far is this end accomplished when the children of families whose parents are of foreign birth or extraction, whose father's occupation is unskilled, or who come from blighted neighborhoods drop out of school and fail to complete more often than those with greater advantages of social status? Evidently, in studies of the effect upon individual adjustment of the number of years of formal education, selective factors are at work. Hence it is too often true that other things are not equal.

In this study an attempt was made to hold constant six factors

[15] Louis Guttman, "A Revision of Chapin's Social Status Scale," *American Sociological Review*, June, 1942, pp. 362–369.

[16] This section appeared originally in an article by F. Stuart Chapin, "A Study of Social Adjustment Using the Technique of Analysis by Selective Control," in *Social Forces*, May, 1940, pp. 476–487.

that would influence eventual economic adjustment if they were allowed to vary. We can therefore say we have measured the effect upon an individual child's adjustment in the community of different durations of high school education, "six other things being equal." Thus, we have tried to face squarely the limitations set by the usual phrase, "other things being equal," because *we have made approximately equal* six factors—father's occupation, parents' nationality, neighborhood status, sex, age in years, and average high school grades. When these factors are not held constant, they may in and of themselves explain differences in eventual economic adjustment that might really be due to differences in length of exposure to the opportunities of high school education. By holding these factors constant as between an experimental group of girls and boys who graduated from a four years' high school course and a control group who left school before graduation, we even up the extraneous factors and bring into relief the two things we wish to measure, the amount of high school education and economic adjustment.

Figure 5 shows in graphic form the shrinkage of cases from the original 2127 to the final 46. This elimination of 2081 cases, or 97.8 per cent, illustrates two difficulties of all such studies: first, the large proportion of cases, 43.8 per cent, or 933, not found for interview in 1935 or inaccessible because of moving away, incomplete records, or death; and second, the large proportion of cases, 54 per cent, or 1148, eliminated in the process of matching on six controls. Stouffer[17] has

[17] S. A. Stouffer and T. S. Lazarsfeld, *The Family in the Depression*, 1937, Social Science Research Council, Bulletin 39, p. 175 and footnote of p. 176. Matching by manual manipulation (hand manipulation), i.e., the sorting out of cases from the two compared groups into classes of a determined range, is a tedious procedure and results in the elimination of many cases owing to inability to match them. This difficulty may be avoided by use of the formula devised by Wilks and by Guttman. See S. S. Wilks, "The Standard Error of the Means of 'Matched Samples,'" *Journal of Educational Psychology*, 1931, pp. 205–208, and "On the Distribution of Statistics in Samples from a Normal Population of Two Variables in Matched Sampling of One Variable," *Metron*, No. 3–4, 1932; also Louis Guttman, "On Uses of the Critical Ratio: A Research Paper," for the M.A. degree, University of Minnesota, June, 1939 (unpublished), especially Section 12, "Differences between Matched Groups" (pp. 29–34), and Section 13, "The Special Case of Matched Individuals" (pp. 35–36). There are empirical advantages, however, that accrue to the student from manual

devised a method of analysis for dealing with cases not found, unknown cases, or refusals, which estimates what could have been the
effect if the unknown cases had shown a certain amount of bias.
Since the Lazarsfeld-Stouffer correction is based on the implicit assumption of a representative sampling procedure and the present
study is one utilizing controls to obtain pure or homogeneous samples, we have not attempted this correction device but confine our
analysis to the 1194 cases interviewed in 1935.

The purpose of the Christiansen study was to isolate the presumed
cause-and-effect relationship between length of exposure to high
school education as a cause (from 1922 to 1926) and economic adjustment as the effect (as found in 1935). To extricate the relationship
between two factors from the usual complex of influences, it was
necessary to control by matching as many factors as possible. As we
have indicated, six factors which, if uncontrolled, might themselves
explain the relationship were held constant as far as this could be
done, considering the fact that each was essentially an unmeasured
factor derived from admittedly inadequate records.

These factors may be listed in two classes. The first consists of

---

manipulation, despite its limitations; for by handling the cases he gets to know
them more thoroughly. Furthermore, the method of manual matching is easier to
explain to the non-mathematical consumer of research results than is matching by
symbolic manipulation in mathematical formulas. In a somewhat different connection,
Ezekiel claims an advantage for freehand curves in his graphic short-cut method for
multiple curvilinear regression, and states on p. 241 of his *Methods of Correlation
Analysis* (John Wiley, 1930), ". . . In fact, the emphasis on critical study of the individual observations is a point in favor of the graphic short-cut method. It forces
the researcher to know his data more thoroughly, and so to exercise thought and care
in working out relations and in interpreting their significance."

In the computation of the standard error of the difference between means of
matched groups allowance can be made for the fact that the process of matching
introduced a degree of correlation. Owing to the crude character of the matching
factors used in the studies herein described, no correction was introduced for this
fact. If the correlation is substantial and positive ($+$), the size of the standard
errors would be reduced, thus increasing the size of the critical ratios and increasing
the statistical significance of the obtained differences. Thus without this correction
the results are conservative and err on the side of safety. For a discussion of this
matter, see C. C. Peters and W. R. Van Vorhees, *Statistical Procedures and Their
Mathematical Bases,* McGraw-Hill, 1940, pp. 162–167, and E. F. Lindquist, *Statistical Analysis in Educational Research,* Houghton Mifflin, 1940, pp. 58–59.

factors of social status, such as: (1) father's occupational class [18]; (2) parents' nationality; (3) neighborhood status.[19] The second class consists of factors of individual difference, such as (4) chronological age; (5) sex; and (6) average of all high school marks.[20]

The test of the effectiveness of these six controls may rest upon the results of applying them. Certainly, as we shall show, the use of these controls did in the third set of samples yield a much more decisive result in favor of the graduates than was found in the first crude control sample. This result indicates that even these few controls were effective in equalizing individual factors and the social status influences favorable at the outset to graduates and unfavorable to non-graduates. We are not, however, here concerned with the problem of causation so much as with an analysis of the technique of using rough non-measured factors and non-measured criteria of effect.

Before passing on to an analysis of the effect on selective criteria of adjustment of the six factors of control, it should be noted that it was not possible to control four additional factors which should be controlled in any repetition of the experiment. We refer to (1) physical health; (2) number of broken homes; (3) exact money income; and (4) persistence. The last factor is quite intangible, although recent studies[21] seem to suggest the possibility of its measurement and it may have an important bearing upon educational achievement and economic adjustment. No doubt other equally important factors of control will occur to the reader, but it should be

[18] Converted into numerical weights in which Class I = 7 points; Class II = 6 points; etc. For composition of the classes, see the Barr-Taussig *Scale of Occupations* in Terman's *Genetic Studies of Genius,* 1925, pp. 66–72.

[19] Ratings of areas of the city of St. Paul by the St. Paul City Planning Engineer on six classes—A, B, C, D, E, and F—converted into arbitrary numerical equivalents: A = 6; B = 5; etc.

[20] Taken as indication of intelligence in the absence of information about the I.Q. and grouped in five classes—A, B, C, D, and E—converted into arbitrary numerical equivalents: A = 93–100; B = 86–92; C = 80–85; D = 75–79; and E = below 74.

[21] E. G. Ryans, "The Major Observable Dimensions of Behavior," *Journal of General Psychology,* July, 1938, pp. 65–96. Also, "The Meaning of Persistence," *ibid.,* pp. 79–96; also, "An Experimental Attempt to Analyze Persistent Behavior," *ibid.,* pp. 333–371.

remembered that this experiment was limited to accessible crude data and is a test of what can be done with these rather than an example of a more ideally scientific study.

Turning now to the question of effect, we are again limited by the availability of criteria of economic adjustment or community adjustment that may be obtained from simple interviews conducted by untrained E.R.A. visitors. With such interviewers, it is not possible to use sociometric scales to measure morale, social participation, or other standardized criteria of adjustment. The criteria of community adjustment used initially were five in number—(1) the number of job changes from 1926 to 1935 which involved salary increases or no change in salary, a probable indication of feelings of security; (2) percentage voting, an indication of interest in political activity and of some confidence in popular government as a device to attain and to maintain social security and adjustment; (3) occupational class attained, an indication of adjustment by climbing the occupational ladder because of the association between social status and individual security; (4) additional years of education after leaving high school; and (5) the number of personal interests in diversified activity. It should be evident that these criteria, although rough, are all matters of fact that could be ascertained by unskilled interviewers.

The need of controls to equalize educational opportunity in any study that purports to isolate cause-and-effect relationship may be shown by the analysis of one example—father's occupational class— since such an analysis will illustrate the point for all factors. Table 16 shows that the graduates had a decided initial advantage in social status because 19.9 per cent of this group had fathers who were professional men and members of the managerial class, compared with only 4.41 per cent of the non-graduates. Similarly, only 10.3 per cent of the graduates had fathers who were laborers or unemployed, whereas 22.37 per cent of the non-graduates had fathers in these classes. To equalize these occupational influences, we present Table 17. Here it will be seen, reading from left to right, that samples of 400 cases and samples of 46 cases—columns (3), (4) and columns (5), (6) respectively—show progressive equalization of the initial

TABLE 16: Evidence of Advantage of Graduates

Father's Occupational Class[a]	1194 Interviewed in 1935			
	Non-Graduates		Graduates	
	Number	Per Cent	Number	Per Cent
I. Professional................	3	0.58	66	9.9
II. Managerial.................	20	3.83	68	10.0
III. Clerical	182	34.79	275	41.2
IV. Skilled operatives	162	30.98	169	25.0
V. Semi-skilled	39	7.45	24	3.6
VI. Laborers	14	2.68	3	0.4
VII. Unemployed	103	19.69	66	9.9
Totals.....................	523	100.00	671	100.00

[a] Based on Barr-Taussig scale in Terman's *Genetic Studies of Genius*, pp. 66–72, with unemployed added as group VII.

TABLE 17. How Cases Are Eliminated When Factors Are Controlled by Matching

Father's Occupational Class	1194 Interviewed in 1935				400 with 5 Factors Controlled				46 with 6 Factors on Precision Control				46 Random Sample			
	523 Non-Graduates (1)		671 Graduates (2)		200 Non-Graduates (3)		200 Graduates (4)		23 Non-Graduates (5)		23 Graduates (6)		23[a] Non-Graduates (7)		23[b] Graduates (8)	
	No.	%	No.	%	No.	%	No.	%	No.	%	No.	%	No.	%	No.	%
I	3	0.58	66	9.9	1	0.5	4	2.0		0		0		0	2	8.7
II	20	3.83	68	10.0	10	5.0	18	9.0	1	4.4	1	4.4	1	4.4	2	8.7
III	182	34.79	275	41.2	94	47.0	94	47.0	12	52.1	12	52.1	13	56.4	11	47.8
IV	162	30.98	169	25.0	74	37.0	73	36.5	8	34.8	8	34.8	8	34.8	6	26.1
V	39	7.45	24	3.6	17	8.5	11	5.5	2	8.7	2	8.7		0	2	8.7
VI	14	2.68	3	0.4	4	2.0		0		0		0	1	4.4		0
VII	103	19.69	66	9.9		0		0		0		0		0		0
Totals	523	100.0	671	100.0	200	100.0	200	100.0	23	100.0	23	100.0	23	100.0	23	100.0

[a] Random sample of 23 non-graduates: every 22nd case selected from an alphabetical list of 523 in column (1).

[b] Random sample of 23 graduates: every 29th case selected from an alphabetical list of 671 in column (2).

Randomness of selection at intervals from an alphabetical list is established by a rank order correlation of Rho = .07 or practically zero, between alphabetical order and order on criterion 1, see Table 20.

disparity. In columns (5) and (6) the factor "father's occupation" is exactly equalized as between the graduate group and the non-graduate group, and, as we shall soon see, this equalizing process due to matching on the occupational factor did, nevertheless, increase the adjustment of the graduate group. But since in this process we equalized on six controls, meanwhile allowing length of high school

TABLE 18.   Analysis of Process of Shrinkage Due to Matching on Controls

Father's Occupational Class	1194 Interviewed in 1935		Cases Eliminated NG = Non-Graduates G = Graduates	46 with 6 Factors Controlled	
	Non-Graduates 523	Graduates 671		Non-Graduates 23	Graduates 23
	Number	Number		Number	Number
I	3	66	3 NG; 66G		
II	20	68	19 NG; 67 G	1	1
III	182	275	170 NG; 263 G	12	12
IV	162	169	154 NG; 161 G	8	8
V	39	24	37 NG; 22 G	2	2
VI	14	3	14 NG; 3 G		
VII	103	66	103 NG; 66 G		
Totals	523	671	1148	23	23

education to vary, we may conclude that the increased adjustment of the graduates is probably due to the fact that they had two more years of high school education than the non-graduates. Table 18 is added merely to show how many cases of graduates or non-graduates were eliminated by the six precise controls in the final small samples of 23 each. It shows more exactly than Figure 5 just how the cases were eliminated by father's occupational class as controls were established. It also shows that the effect of controls was to truncate the distribution of these factors.

Let us now turn to the effective controls on criteria of community adjustment. Table 19 shows the differences between non-graduates and graduates on the five criteria of adjustment for which comparable information was secured. It is evident that in every one of the three matched comparisons in columns (1), (2), and (3), the graduates (experimental group) had a higher percentage or a higher average score than the non-graduates.[22] To render the data

TABLE 19.   Differences between Non-Graduates and Graduates on Five Criteria of Community Adjustment

Criteria of Community Adjustment	(1) Five Control Samples		(2) Six Control Samples		(3) Six Precise Control Samples		(4) Random Samples	
	200 Non-Graduates; Average 1.99 Yrs. Ed.	200 Graduates; Average 4 Yrs. Ed.	145 Non-Graduates; Average 2 Yrs. Ed.	145 Graduates; Average 4 Yrs. Ed.	23 Non-Graduates; Average 2.13 Yrs. Ed.	23 Graduates; Average 4 Yrs. Ed.	23 Non-Graduates; Average 1.9 Yrs. Ed.	23 Graduates; Average 4 Yrs. Ed.
1. Salary, per cent increase or no change........	78.0	85.4	83.4	88.7	58.0	92.0	75.0	88.0
Index...........	100	109	100	106	100	158	100	117
Gain...........		9		6		58		17
2. Voting, per cent....	76.0	85.5	75.0	88.0	82.6	86.9	87.0	78.0
Index...........	100	112	100	117	100	105	100	89
Gain...........		12		17		5		−11
3. Occupation class of student.......	4.41	5.41	4.36	5.07	4.69	4.95	4.34	5.13
Index...........	100	122	100	116	100	105	100	118
Gain...........		22		16		5		18
4. Average added years of education ...	0.695	1.450	0.69	1.40	0.87	1.52	0.82	1.22
Index...........	100	208	100	203	100	174	100	148
Gain...........		108		103		74		48
5. Average number of interests.......	0.60	0.91	0.60	0.82	1.00	1.13	0.78	0.91
Index...........	100	151	100	136	100	113	100	116
Gain...........		51		36		13		16

more comparable, the percentage or score of the non-graduates was taken as 100 and the indicia of the graduates reduced to this base. Thus in column (1), 78 per cent of the 200 non-graduates (control group) had salary increases, or no change in salary from 1926 to 1935 in the aggregate job changes experienced in this interval, but of the 200 graduates (experimental group), 85.4 per cent, or 7.4 per cent more, had this favorable experience. If, then, we take 78 per cent as a base equal to 100, the 85.4 per cent becomes 109,

[22] The only instance of loss on the part of graduates occurs in the random sample comparisons of column (4), row 2, which will be analyzed later.

or a gain of 9 points on this index. Similarly, the mean occupational score of 4.41 as 100 gives to the score 5.41 an index value of 122, or a gain of 22 points on this index. Thus, by converting each comparison into an index, we can sum up the differences or gains of the graduate group on all of the five criteria in the form of numerical indicia. This conversion greatly facilitates comparison. It will be observed that the advantage of the graduate group ranges from 5 to 108 points, fluctuates on several criteria, and does not always yield the greatest advantage to the samples (3) in which precise control by identical individual matching was used. Furthermore, the most violent fluctuations of indicia occur on criteria 4 and 5. Obviously, these criteria are less stable. Critical appraisal of criterion 4, average years of education after leaving high school, indicates that this criterion gives automatic advantage to the graduate group, since a high school diploma is, itself, often a *sine qua non* for admission to further education. We shall, therefore, eliminate this criterion from future comparisons. Critical appraisal of criterion 5, average number of interests, diminishes confidence in this type of evidence because of the crude nature of the inquiry about interests made by untrained visitors. This criterion also will henceforth be dropped from our analysis.

Having eliminated criteria 4 and 5, we now turn to Table 20, in which we may examine the comparisons of summations of indicia on criteria 1, 2, and 3 for all samples. Table 20 is based upon the more dependable and objective criteria of economic and community adjustment: (1) percentage of jobs showing salary increase or no change; (2) percentage voting; and (3) occupational class score of subject. This table also enables us to analyze the relative effect of the number of controls and the precision of these controls in relation to a tentative norm of random samples.

Scores of 21 points on criteria 1 and 2 and of 43 points on criteria 1, 2, and 3 of column (1) are the summation of indicia after matching frequency distributions simultaneously on five controls applied. Comparison of indicia sums of 23 points and 39 points in column (2) shows that the addition of one more control (now six controls in all), that is, by matching frequency distributions on average high school marks, does not yield any significant gain or loss. But now examine column (3), wherein six controls (age, sex, parents' nationality, neighborhood status, father's occupation, high school marks) are applied by the more precise method of identical individual matching. At once, the sums of indicia increase in striking degree—that is, the

TABLE 20. Summation of Differences between Non-Graduates and Graduates Converted into Indicia of Criteria of Community Adjustment

Criteria of Community Adjustment Expressed as Sums of Indicia	(1) Five Control Samples	(2) Six Control Samples	(3) Six Precise Control Samples	(4) Random Samples

1. Sum 1 and 2
  1 = Salary criterion.........
  2 = Voting criterion.........
	21	23	63	6

2. Sum 1, 2, and 3
  1 = Salary criterion.........
  2 = Voting criterion.........
  3 = Occupational criterion......
	43	39	68	24

63 points on two criteria (row 1), and 68 points on three criteria (row 2), increases of 173 per cent and 74 per cent, respectively. Similarly, the effect of precision of control on comparisons with corresponding indicia of random samples, shown in column (4), is to yield a differential of 57 points on criteria 1 and 2, and of 44 points on criteria 1, 2, and 3, or differences of 950 per cent and 183 per cent respectively.[23]

[23] The random samples of column (4), Table 20, were obtained as indicated in the footnote to Table 17. The purpose of taking a random sample of 23 non-graduates from the 523 interviewed and of 23 graduates from the 671 interviewed was to provide for purposes of comparison with the control samples of 23 each, two groups of equal size but representing unselected cases as a norm of the differences to expect on chance occurrence. This enables us to apply useful theoretical criteria of probability as an additional test of significance to the simpler tests of mere absolute size.

These facts establish the principle for this experiment, at least, that precision of control is more effective in the isolation of probable causal relationship between length of high school education and degree of economic adjustment than mere number of crude controls by matching frequency distributions. Precision of controls in sample (3) was obtained by identical individual matching, which means that for every boy in the non-graduate group of 23 cases there is another boy in the graduate group with the same father's occupational class, the same parents' nationality, from a home in the same neighborhood, of the same age, and with the same average high school marks. The same matching procedure applies to girls. It is evident that these stringent conditions for equalizing differences on six controls are so severe that 244 cases are eliminated because they cannot meet one or more of these conditions.

Let us now examine more carefully some of the subtler implications of the technique used in constructing Table 20, since this one table is the chief evidence for the contention that cause-and-effect relationships have been partially isolated by means of comparatively crude controls and factual criteria.

It is evident that the differences between columns (3) and (4) of row 1 (that is to say, 63 points compared to 6 in Table 20) are accounted for by the plus 34 per cent advantage of graduates—Table 19, column (3), row 1—in the precisely controlled sample, and by the minus 9 per cent disadvantage of graduates in the random sample—Table 19, column (4), row 2. Since our argument in justification of the utility of precise controls rests on these two data, it becomes necessary to inquire whether the differences of plus 34 per cent in one case and minus 9 per cent in the other case, which are the raw differences that underlie the large differences in indicia, are statistically reliable. An answer to this question is found by calculating the probability of such differences occurring by chance.

Is the difference of plus 34 per cent likely to occur often in small random samples as a chance fluctuation? If so, such a difference is not significant. But exactly how often would such a difference, or a slightly larger one, occur in random sampling? It would occur once in about 200 trials.[24] Chance occurrence is therefore rare. Hence, when it occurs in practice, the odds are about 200 to 1 against such a difference occurring by chance, and we regard its occurrence as significant. Correspondingly, in the random sample for a difference of minus 9 per cent, the chances of such a difference are 1 in 14, or about 13 against 1 of such an occurrence by chance.[25] Since, in the comparison, an occurrence of minus 9 per cent is sufficiently frequent by chance so that when it occurs in practice it cannot be regarded as significant, we may therefore conclude that the positive advantage, plus 34 per cent of the graduates in the precision sample, is a reliable difference and that the negative position, minus 9 per cent of the graduates in the random sample, is not a reliable difference. By this line of reasoning, we find the theoretical support for our contention that the differences among indicia in Table 20, columns (3) and (4), establish the utility of precise controls in this kind of analysis. Of course, we have only the evidence of one experiment. More adequate proof requires verification by repetition of this type of experiment.

Let us now examine more minutely the two distinct criteria of economic adjustment, salary change and student's present occupational class. Table 21 shows the variation and percentage, salary increases and job changes, and the percentage experiencing no change and the percentage with salary increases. It will be observed that the large samples, (1) and (2), show more decisive gradation with years of educational exposure than the precise control sample (3), in which the fluctuations are more pronounced, as is usually the case in small samples. When, however, the totals of all non-graduates, whether with one or two or three years of high school attendance, are thrown together and the percentage is recomputed

[24] The critical ratio of the difference of 34 per cent between the non-graduate group and the graduate group is 2.83 by the following formula:

$$S.D._{(p_2 - p_1)} = \sqrt{\left(\frac{N_1 + N_2}{N_1 + N_2 - 2}\right)\left(\frac{p_1 q_1}{N_2} + \frac{p_2 q_2}{N_1}\right)}$$

being an adaption of Fischer's "t" formula to the standard deviation of a proportion.

[25] The critical ratio of the difference of minus 9 per cent between the non-graduate group and the graduate group of the random sample, by the same formula, is $- 0.18$.

for comparison with all graduates, we find that only 58 per cent had salary increases or no change in salary, compared with 92 per cent (the sum of 54 and 38) of the graduate group. Thus, although the samples (1) of 200 cases each show a regular gain in economic adjustment with each additional year of education—column (1)—

TABLE 21. Economic Adjustment. Per Cent Changes in Jobs, 1926–1935, with Salary Increases, No Change, or Decreases

Left High School in 1926 After	Per Cent Salary Increases [a]			Per Cent Salary, No Change [a]			Per Cent Salary Decreases		
	(1) 5— Control Samples $N = 400$	(2) 6— Control Samples $N = 290$	(3) 6— Control Samples $N = 46$	(1) 5— Control Samples $N = 400$	(2) 6— Control Samples $N = 290$	(3) 6— Control Samples $N = 46$	(1) 5— Control Samples $N = 400$	(2) 6— Control Samples $N = 290$	(3) 6— Control Samples $N = 46$
1 year's attendance........	28.4	25.9	33.3	42.0	48.2	25.0	29.6	25.9	41.6
2 years' attendance........	38.4	46.3	26.7	39.5	38.8	40.0	21.9	14.9	33.3
3 years' attendance........	47.7	56.8	31.2	37.2	32.8	18.7	15.1	10.4	50.0
4 years' attendance, graduates........	55.1	53.2	54.0	30.3	35.5	38.0	14.6	11.3	8.0

[a] In this table the sum 55.1 (per cent salary increases) and 30.3 (per cent no salary change), of the 200 graduates (bottom row) is 85.4 per cent, which appears in Table 19, column (1), row 1. Nongraduates added together and per cent for this group of 200 recomputed in Table 19, column (1), row 1.

the dichotomous comparison for the small samples (3) yields an even more favorable test for the graduate group. This evidence justifies dependence on criterion 1, salary increase or no salary change during 1926–1935, as a test of the techniques used in this controlled analysis.

On the other hand, the criterion of student's occupation in 1935 is not as satisfactory. Table 22 shows that the occupational class differences in favor of the graduates fluctuate from 23.3 per cent for professional and managerial occupations in the 1194 original group to 21.5 per cent in samples (1), to 15.6 per cent in samples (2), and a rise to 22.1 per cent in samples (3). Thus the control of factors does not seem to enhance the effectiveness of the occupational criterion. For this reason, we conclude that row 1 of Table 20 applies the best test of the utility of this experiment and establishes more decisively than the sum of three criteria the effects of precision of control on six factors.

TABLE 22. Analysis of Percentage Differences between Non-Graduates and Graduates on Criterion of Student's Occupational Class

Occupational Class of Students	Original 1194 Interviewed in 1935			(1) Five Control Samples			(2) Six Control Samples			(3) Six Precise Control Samples		
	523 Non-Graduates	671 Graduates	Differences	200 Non-Graduates	200 Graduates	Differences	145 Non-Graduates	145 Graduates	Differences	23 Non-Graduates	23 Graduates	Differences
I	2.3	19.8	+17.5	4.0	16.0	+12.0	4.0	13.1	+9.1	4.4	17.8	+13.4
II	4.5	10.3	+5.8	3.5	13.0	+9.5	3.6	13.1	+6.5	0	8.7	+8.7
III	47.1	48.0	+0.9	46.0	49.0	+3.0	48.2	53.1	+4.8	65.2	39.1	−26.1
IV	32.1	12.0	−20.1	33.0	16.5	−16.5	29.0	15.2	−14.8	21.7	26.0	+4.3
V	4.9	2.3	−2.6	6.0	2.0	−4.0	5.5	2.1	−3.4	8.7	4.4	−4.3
VI	3.0	0.8	−2.2	4.5	1.0	−3.5	3.6	1.4	−2.2	0	4.4	+4.4
VII	6.1	6.8	+0.7	3.0	2.5	−0.5	6.1	2.0	−4.1	0	0	0
	100.0	100.0		100.0	100.0		100.0	100.0		100.0	100.0	

Since this conclusion limits the test of the experiment to only two criteria, namely (1) per cent salary increases or no changes, and (2) per cent voting, we turn finally to Table 23, and consider the probability of differences of specified size between percentages occurring by chance. Taking the percentages found in the random samples as a norm for comparison with the small samples having precision control on six factors, we may ask whether the difference of 21 per cent between the 34 per cent advantage of the graduates in the control sample and the 13 per cent advantage of graduates in the random sample is a difference or gain that frequently occurs by chance. The last column shows that the approximate critical ratio is 6.04 for a 21 per cent difference in advantage on criterion 1. Since, by probability tables,[26] the odds of such occurrence by chance

[26] H. Arkin and R. C. Colton, *An Outline of Statistical Methods*, 1938, pp. 114 and 120. The approximation critical ratio formula for a difference between gains is

$$C.R. = (\bar{v}_2 - \bar{v}_1) \sqrt{\frac{N(N-1)}{(p_1'q_1' + p_1q_1 + p_2'q_2' + p_2q_2)}}, \text{ when } N_1 = N_2.$$

This formula is adopted for use in dealing with proportions from formula (5) by Louis Guttman, in "On Uses of the Critical Ratio," p. 26, a research paper for M.A. degree, University of Minnesota, June, 1939.

are approximately only 1 in 500,000,000 trials, we may conclude that this difference is highly significant. Similarly, the approximate critical ratio for a difference of 15.3 is 4.53, with odds of 1 in over 2000 of

TABLE 23. Analysis of Probability of Occurrence of a Difference between Differences on Criteria of Salary and Voting

Criterion of Adjustment	6 Precise Control Samples		Random Samples		Differences of Differences	
	Non-Graduates	Graduates	Non-Graduates	Graduates	Difference of Per Cent	Critical Ratio
1. Salary, per cent increase or no change......	58.0	92.0	75.0	88.0		
Difference.....		34.0		13.0	21.0	6.04 [a]
2. Voting, per cent	82.6	86.9	82.0	78.0		
Difference.....		4.3		−11.0	15.3	4.53 [a]

[a] In this table we assume that the proportions and the differences found for the random samples on each criterion represent the normal differences between non-graduates and graduates. Then the greater differences found for the controlled comparisons may be interpreted as differentials isolated by controlled analysis and their statistical significance tested as above.

such a difference occurring by chance. Therefore, this difference is also highly significant.[27]

The entire analysis may now be summarized under six main points:

1. Simple factual records may yield highly significant differences that test a cause-and-effect hypothesis, provided a large number of cases are used at the outset (2127 in this study) and a long period intervenes between cause and effect (nine years in this study).

2. The elimination of cases is very heavy in a long-time study and especially as the number and precision of controls increase.

3. Simple factual data gathered by untrained interviewers may yield significant results when the control group technique is used.

4. Making the controls precise by identical individual matching

[27] Again we call the reader's attention to the fact that in chap. VII there is a discussion of the limitations imposed by the application of the conventional probability tests derived from random samples to such cases of non-random samples as experimental and control groups used in the experimental designs of this book.

on the factors available is much more effective than mere number of controls used without precision.

5. Recently devised formulas for computing the critical ratio of differences among proportions in samples provide a test of the probability of occurrence of these differences by chance.

6. The techniques developed in this ex post facto experiment seem sufficiently successful in isolating probable cause-and-effect relationships to suggest that they provide an additional method of research in longitudinal studies of human behavior.

RENTALS AND TUBERCULOSIS DEATH RATES IN NEW YORK CITY [28]

In the two preceding applications of ex post facto experimental design some present effect of a social program upon individuals or families was traced back to an earlier date when this program began operating as a cause, or as a means to achieve some desired end. In both instances the *same individuals and families* were compared over the experimental period. In the study now to be described an attempt was made to apply this experimental design in an analysis of assumed cause-and-effect relationships in which the units studied were not the same individuals or families but the populations residing in the *same areas* for the experimental period. Consequently this study is in human ecology and presents the results of an exploration of the possibilities of analysis of cause-and-effect relations in a field of social phenomena hitherto investigated by different methods. It is hoped that the results will be regarded as sufficiently definitive to encourage further application of the method to other ecological relationships in which causal factors are postulated as antecedent to some present effect, so that our understanding of human relations may extend and deepen.

Are high standards of housing in 1930 related to lowered tuberculosis death rates in 1940? Is it possible in the use of analysis by experimental design to isolate the antecedent influence of a complex of housing factors upon the tuberculosis death rate of a later date?

[28] In this study the author acknowledges the assistance of three graduate students, Toimi E. Kyllonen, John N. Burrus, and Marvin J. Taves, in a graduate seminar at the University of Minnesota during the year 1945–1946.

To test the possibilities of finding an answer to these questions a large city (universe of small areas) was selected in which the decline in tuberculosis death rates 1931–1940 was, on the average, not significant [29] except as a small segment of a long-time trend. Then a group of low tuberculosis death rate areas of 1940 was compared with a group of high tuberculosis death rate areas of 1940, by tracing back to 1930 for each area the magnitude of the mean monthly rentals (taken as a rough measure of a bundle of interrelated housing factors).

The results of this analysis by ex post facto experimental design are as follows: (1) a decline in tuberculosis death rates of high statistical significance [30] from 1931 to 1940 was *preceded* by high standards of housing in 1930; and (2) a decline in the tuberculosis death rates of non-statistical significance [31] from 1931 to 1940 was preceded by low standards of housing in 1930. Thus the conclusion seems justified that high housing standards precede a decline in tuberculosis death rates, but that low housing standards in areas studied are not related to a decline in tuberculosis death rates.

The foregoing brief summary of results now requires detailed explanation of the sequence of operations performed to obtain them: (1) a description of the universe of study and the samples drawn from it; (2) definition of high and low housing standards; (3) description of the procedures in an ex post facto experimental design; (4) statement of variations from former procedure in this design; (5) limitations and weaknesses of this study; and (6) possibilities of further application of this method of analysis of social relationships.

The Universe and the Samples

There were 354 health areas in New York City for which in 1940 comparable data were recorded: (1) the tuberculosis death rates per

[29] A critical ratio of change in tuberculosis death rates from a stratified random sample, 1931–1940, was 0.59.

[30] The critical ratio of change in tuberculosis death rates in high rent areas was 4.6.

[31] The critical ratio of change in tuberculosis death rates in low rent areas was 1.90.

100,000 of population (X_1);[32] (2) median monthly rentals (X_5); (3) percentage of population native white (X_3); and (4) percentage of population colored (X_4). These health areas are the universe from which samples for 1940 were drawn.

To obtain the greatest contrast in tuberculosis death rates the 354 health areas were put in array on these rates for 1940 and the upper quartile of areas $(N = 88)$ was chosen for comparison with the lower quartile areas $(N = 88)$. These two samples from the extremes of the distribution of tuberculosis death rates—shown in Table 24, column (3), rows 1 and 4—were matched by frequency distributions on percentage native white (X_3), and percentage colored (X_4). In this process of equating by frequencies, 47 health areas were eliminated from each group because they could not be matched. The remaining 41 high tuberculosis rate areas are hereinafter called the "experimental group" and the 41 low rate areas are called the "control group." (See Table 24, rows 2 and 3.)

Since it was desirable to obtain a norm to which the experimental group and the control group could be compared, a stratified random sample of 42 health areas was selected from the 354 areas of New York City in 1940 as follows: The stratification was by city boroughs, i.e., the data for each health area having been recorded on a separate card, these cards were grouped by boroughs; then each group of cards was shuffled by one person while another took out every seventh card in each borough group; in this manner the stratified random sample mentioned above was obtained.

---

[32] Actually the tuberculosis rate data are the mean rates of 1931 to 1935 taken as 1931 and the mean rates of 1936 to 1940 taken as 1940. See Bellows, Drolet, Goode, and Widdemer, *Neighborhood Health Development, Health Center Districts,* Department of Health, City of New York, Handbook, Statistical Reference Data, Ten-Year Period, 1931–1940. Bellows, Drolet, Goode, and Widdemer report the existence in 1940 of 354 health areas in New York City. However, they record comparable data for 1930 and 1940 for only 306 of these areas. In the present study, the 354 health areas have been considered the universe; a quartile then consists of 88 of these areas. These 88 cases have been selected from the 306 areas for which comparable 1930 and 1940 data are actually available. The quartile here reported thus represents more than 25 per cent of the 306 areas on which the study must be based. The net effect upon the results is to give a more conservative picture than is actually true, since these "quartiles" are "closer" to each other than true quartiles would be.

TABLE 24. Contrasting Tuberculosis Death Rates in Contrasting Rental Areas, New York City, 1930–1940

Contrasting Areas	1930		1940	
	TB Rates	Rentals	TB Rates	Rentals
	(1)	(2)	(3)	(4)
1. Upper quartile on TB rates..........	115.45	$39.88	106.45	$29.88
2. Experimental group	96.96	$36.65	83.97	$28.80
3. Control group.....	32.00	$72.48	22.63	$48.41
4. Lower quartile on TB rates..........	32.11	$70.61	11.15	$46.65

Definition of High and Low Housing Standards

Median monthly rentals (X_5) for each health area were taken as a rough index of housing conditions for 1930 and 1940. Other indices of housing standards of greater validity would have been preferable to median rentals, but *it needs to be remembered that rentals were the only recorded index of housing for these areas available to us.* Thus the index of housing standards although admittedly weak would, if the results were significant despite an imperfect index, yield conclusions which would be at least conservative as compared with the probable results of a more perfect index of housing conditions.

The results of other studies (based on other areas) of the relationship between rentals and housing factors show that rentals are often correlated with tuberculosis death rates, the percentage crowded, the income of the family, etc. For example, Schmid[33] found a correlation of $r = -.532$ with tuberculosis death rates, of $r = -.555$ with percentage crowded, and that this latter correlation persisted, i.e., did not drop below $-.40$, despite partialing out other

[33] Based upon 450 enumeration districts of the Twin Cities, *Social Saga of Two Cities*, 1935.

variables such as percentage needing major repairs, percentage of dwelling units without central heat, percentage of structures 35 years of age and older, percentage of one-family structures, and percentage without gas. Furthermore, he found a multiple correlation of .743 between rental and overcrowding and mean value of structure. Britten [34] found an increase in the relative prevalence of secondary tuberculosis cases for all ages under 65 years of age with increase in room-crowding, age, and income controlled. The increases were most closely associated for tuberculosis cases 15 years of age and under. *The Minnesota Income Study* of 1938–1939 reports a correlation of .678 between rentals and income. A study of the Housing Authority of the City of New Haven of 17 families with a tubercular history and resident in the public housing development showed a favorable prognosis in 15 of the 17 cases, whereas a control group of 17 families matched on significant factors showed only 9 families with favorable prognosis.[35] These findings are the basis for the assumption made in this study that rentals are a rough index of a bundle of related housing factors. We assume, therefore, that high rentals are a partial index of high housing conditions, and vice versa.

The Procedure of Ex Post Facto Experimental Design

In the present study tuberculosis death rates of 1940 were taken as the dependent or effect variable and the health areas recording these rates were studied in 1930 for variations in rentals, taken as the independent variable or complex of causal factors.[36] Obviously such a study is strictly limited by available records of present and past events or trends, since no new measures of past events can be made in the present. Hence the causal factors are likely to be far fewer than one would wish them to be and are much more limited than in the projected experimental design wherein a follow-up to some future date is contemplated. Furthermore, the controls available may

[34] *American Journal of Public Health,* February, 1942, Fig. 2, based on data of the National Health Survey of 1935–1936.

[35] *Journal of Housing,* December, 1945–January, 1946.

[36] This complex of antecedent causal factors consists of the combination of the unplanned consequences of many independently planned social actions, or, to state the matter briefly, economic forces.

be less numerous and precision of control less easy. Hence in the present analysis the dependent or effect variable (X_1), is the tuberculosis death rates of 1940. The independent variable we desire to test or measure, in both concomitant and prior variation with the tuberculosis death rate, as the assumed causal variable or complex of factors, is median rentals (X_5).

In the present study, the order of procedure from a chosen effect $(X_1 = \text{TB death rates})$ to an assumed cause $(X_5 = \text{rentals})$ was followed. An alternate procedure in ex post facto experimental design is from a chosen causal factor $(X_5 = \text{rentals})$ to an assumed effect $(X_1 = \text{TB death rates})$. One of the authors, Mr. Taves, tried out this second order of procedure [37] on the same New York City data. It was found that comparison of a group of low rent areas $(N = 36)$ in 1930, matched by frequency distribution on percentage colored in 1930, showed in 1940 rates of tuberculosis which diminished 13.3 per cent for the low rent areas of 1930 and 20.9 per cent for the "medium" rent areas of 1930, the former decline having a critical ratio of 1.3 and the latter a critical ratio of 2.8. These results are consistent with the results of the first method, but less decisive, because the rent groups (low and medium) were of less extreme magnitudes than were the tuberculosis death rates used in the first comparison.

Now there are two other variables recorded for the New York City health areas which are known by previous studies to be related to the tuberculosis death rate; these are the percentage native white and the percentage colored in the population. Green [38] found a high relation between a measure of economic conditions (monthly rental and possession of radio and telephone) and the tuberculosis death rate for the four-year period 1928–1931 in 252 census tracts in Cleveland. For whites the tuberculosis rate ranged from 19 in high economic status areas to 127 in the lowest economic status areas, and the rates for Negroes were five times the white rates in each area.

[37] This supplementary analysis is what Greenwood (*op. cit.,* pp. 64–68, and chap. 9) calls ex post facto cause-to-effect experiments, a process of operations in reverse to the sequence followed in the three studies herein summarized.

[38] *Tuberculosis and Economic Strata, Cleveland's Five-City Area, 1928–31,* the Anti-Tuberculosis League, Cleveland, 1931.

Whitney [39] found the tuberculosis rate highest where the living standards were lowest in a study of tuberculosis death rates by occupational groups in several states.

In the present study this same inverse relationship between tuberculosis death rates and economic factors (median rentals) and race (colored) was also found.

Table 24 shows that high tuberculosis death rates (rows 1 and 2) occur where mean rentals are low, and low tuberculosis death rates occur where mean rentals are high (rows 3 and 4). These results are derived from a comparison of extreme rate areas. What is the relationship for the city as a whole? Taking the stratified random sample for an answer to this question we find that the correlation between median rentals [40] and the tuberculosis death rate is $r = .308$, and between percentage native white and tuberculosis rates is $r = -.930$; both results are thus consistent with former findings.

Since, however, a correlation between tuberculosis death rates and median rentals, $r_{15} = -.308$, in the stratified random sample is lower than Schmid's result of $r = -.532$, one wonders whether the relationship found in the stratified random sample for New York City is masked by the larger colored population there than in the Twin Cities studied by Schmid. To test this point the partial correlation in the stratified random sample between the tuberculosis death rate and median rentals was computed, holding constant the percentage colored. [41] The effect was at once striking, since the partial correlation was $r_{15.4} = -.66$, or double the magnitude of the zero order correlation, $r_{15} = -.308$.

It appears, therefore, that control of percentage colored is desirable if the housing factor (rentals) is to be partially isolated. Thus the much higher partial correlation on the effect variable [42] gives us the

[39] *Death Rates by Occupation,* based on data of the U. S. Census Bureau, 1930. National Tuberculosis Association, 1934.

[40] When mean rentals are cited in this paper, the figure is the mean of median rentals for each health area, and correlations are based on recorded median rentals, whereas critical ratios are based on means of these medians.

[41] Of the two nationality and racial factors, the percentage colored is the more important factor, since $r_{15.4} = -.66$.

[42] In another study of infant mortality and median rentals for the same areas, the partial correlation from a stratified random sample increased to $r_{12.34} = -.33$, from

raison d'être for the selection of matching factors (to be held constant) which are to be used in the construction of an experimental group and a control group as we attempt to trace back from 1940 [43] to 1930 with the purpose of discovering an assumed cause-and-effect relationship operating in and by the rentals of 1930.

We are now ready to consider the tabulated figures upon which the conclusions are based which were stated at the beginning of this section.

Table 25 is arranged to show in descending magnitude the tuberculosis death rates of the different samples from the top to the bottom of the table. It will be observed that one effect of matching the upper quartile with the lower quartile on percentage native white and colored is to diminish the range in both tuberculosis rates and mean rentals. The stratified random sample stands in a middle position (row 3) on all rates, which was to be expected. It will be noted also that the critical ratios of changes in rates from 1930 to 1940 (column 5) are non-significant for the tuberculosis death rates in high rate but low rental areas (rows 1 and 2), as also for the stratified random sample (row 3); but that the changes in tuberculosis rates in the low rate areas of high rentals (rows 4 and 5) are highly significant, the critical ratios being all in excess of 4. Further examination of the high tuberculosis rate areas (row 2) shows that the rentals dropped non-significantly (less than 3 standard errors) from $36.65 to $28.80 in 1930–1940, whereas in the control group of low tuberculosis rate and high rent areas (row 4) there was a significant decline (4.2) in rentals from $72.48 in 1930 to $48.41 in 1940. The important point to note is that, despite this decline of significance in rentals for the high rent areas 1930 to 1940, the level of rentals for these areas was even at its lowest value

---

$r_{12} = -.24$, where $X_2 =$ infant mortality, and subsequent analysis by ex post facto experimental design yielded definite but less convincing results than in the tuberculosis-rental study; all of which indicates the value of pre-test by partial correlation.

[43] The constancy of control on percentage colored set in 1940 was maintained for the same areas in 1930; the mean percentage colored in the experimental group was 1.48 per cent in 1940 and 1.7 per cent in 1930, and in the control group was 0.78 per cent in 1940 and 0.65 per cent in 1930.

TABLE 25.   Comparison of All Samples for Tuberculosis Death Rates [a] per 100,000 Population and Means of Median Rentals for 1930 to 1940, New York City Health Areas

Samples	1930		1940		Critical Ratios of Changes
	TB Rates	Rentals	TB Rates	Rentals	
	(1)	(2)	(3)	(4)	(5)
1. Upper quartile, N = 88	115.45	$39.88	106.46	$29.88	−1.21 −8.99
2. Experimental group, N = 41	96.96	$36.65	83.87	$28.80	−1.90 −2.40
3. Stratified random sample, N = 42	55.30	$53.86	50.24	$37.54	−0.59 −5.14
4. Control group, N = 41	32.0	$72.48	22.63	$48.41	−4.6 −4.2
5. Lower quartile, N = 88	32.11	$70.61	22.15	$46.65	−5.28 −7.15
7. United States [b]	67.8		45.9	$27.31	———

[a] All tuberculosis death rates in the 1930 column are for 1931; but rentals are for 1930. Tuberculosis death rates for the United States were obtained from *Vital Statistics Rates in the United States*, 1900–1940, Bureau of the Census, 1943, Table 14, p. 248. Rentals are based on medians and for the United States are from *Statistical Abstract of the United States*, 1944–1945, Table 460, p. 423, and Table 989, p. 912.

[b] Data on the decline in rentals for the United States are not very satisfactory. The general cost of living index for rent in 1930 was 98, and for 1940 was 96. This slight decline may be merely a fluctuation in trend, it may represent a deterioration in housing due to the decline in building, or it may represent a deflationary trend.

($48.41) in excess of the highest rent in the low rent areas ($36.65); thus there was no overlap between the ranges of mean rentals of the experimental and control groups. Evidently a very high and consistently maintained high level of rentals must exist to be associated with a significant decline in tuberculosis death rates; low rentals, despite their decline, are not associated with a significant decline in tuberculosis death rates. Finally, the stratified random sample (row 3) shows that a decline in rentals (from $53.86 to $37.54) is not accompanied by a significant decline in tuberculosis rates.[44]

The assumed cause-and-effect relationship between high rentals and the decline in tuberculosis death rate is measured in terms of the statistical significance of the *change* from 1930 to 1940 in rates. But what *differences* between rates occur for each date singly? Table 26 (taken from rows 2 and 4 of Table 25) shows the statistical

TABLE 26. Differences between Tuberculosis Death Rates and Rentals, Experimental and Control Groups, 1930–1940

Group	1930		1940	
	TB Rates	Rentals	TB Rates	Rentals
	(1)	(2)	(3)	(4)
1. Experimental or high TB rate group	96.96	$36.65	83.87	$28.80
2. Control or low TB rate group........	32.00	$72.48	22.63	$48.41
Differences..........	64.96	$35.83	61.24	$19.61
Critical ratios of differences.........	13.6	6.5	13.3	5.9

significance of differences between tuberculosis rates and rentals of each group for a given date, 1930 or 1940. It will be observed that for tuberculosis rates the critical ratio of 13.3 obtained for 1940 remained constant in 1930, when it was 13.6; similarly the critical ratios of the differences between rentals remained practically constant. These evidences show that throughout the experiment the differences between the groups compared were of the same order. When the same comparison is made between the upper and the lower quartiles, the differences remain highly significant but not constant in terms of the critical ratios, a variation which is probably the result of matching.

[44] The decline in the tuberculosis death rate in the stratified sample paralleled the decline in the tuberculosis rate for the United States as a whole.

New Variations in Technique Introduced in This Study

Two applications of statistical method introduced in this analysis may be noted: (1) selection of a stratified random sample from the universe to serve as a model or norm of probability for changes in rates on the independent and the dependent variables; and (2) use of partial correlation on this sample to discover the probable efficacy of specific control factors for subsequent matching.

In any experimental design the criterion of the significance of *differences between* or *changes in* rates is an estimate of the probable frequency of occurrence of such a change by chance fluctuations of random sampling. The argument runs thus: When the magnitude of the obtained difference or change in rates is one that could occur once in 100 trials (or even less frequently) in random sampling, then the obtained difference or change may be regarded as probably significant of a real difference. Now the practical difficulty with this argument is that the differences or changes in rates obtained are derived from extreme groups matched on control factors and hence not random samples. All that can be said, therefore, is that the changes in rates obtained in this study are of no greater magnitude than might occur had two random samples been chosen and a comparison made between them rather than between an experimental group and a control group. This limitation may be offset in part by selecting a stratified random sample and computing the statistical significance of changes in this sample between the two dates. Since one stratified random sample is for all practical purposes as likely to represent the universe as are two or more random samples, the stratified random sample may serve as a rough norm for comparison. Table 25 (row 3) shows that the stratified random sample does indeed serve as such a norm of probability for measures of statistical significance in approximation studies of the present sort; it serves as such a norm by showing that a change in tuberculosis death rates of 5.06 per 100,000 (from 55.30 in 1930 to 50.24 in 1940) can occur frequently in sampling (critical ratio of 0.59); but that a change of $16.32 in rentals (from $53.86 in 1930 to $37.54 in 1940) occurs very infrequently in sampling (critical ratio of 5.14);

consequently the 13.09 change in tuberculosis rates (from 96.96 in 1930 to 83.87 in 1940) in the experimental group is seen to be non-significant as compared with absolute changes in the corresponding rates of the stratified random sample; and for the control group of high rent areas the decline of 9.37 in tuberculosis rates (from 32.0 in 1930 to 22.63 in 1940) is highly significant as compared with the absolute changes registered in the stratified random sample.[45]

In using the norm of probability, the definition of probability as the limit of relative frequency, or the measure of relative frequency, is used in this section. Such a definition follows the practice of Carnap, Peirce, Venn, and Von Mises,[46] rather than the definitions of meaning of Laplace[47] or of Keynes,[48] which have been sharply distinguished from the former by Carnap and Nagel.

Another consideration now deserves attention: Are the factors chosen for control by matching really functional factors? Here the use of partial correlation on the stratified random sample supplies an empirical answer. If we hold constant one or more accessible factors and obtain an increase in the magnitude of the relationship assumed in the original working hypothesis, namely, that rentals and tuberculosis death rates are related, then symbolic manipulative control by sorting or matching on these factors is likely to be worth while. This was indeed the case since $r_{15} = -.306$ increased to $r_{15.4} = -.66$. On the other hand, when the increase is slight, as in a similar study of the relationship between rentals and infant mortality in New York City health areas, as from $r_{12} = -.24$ to $r_{12.34} = -.33$ (see footnote 42), then symbolic manipulative control of these factors is less likely to isolate the real relationship. In this

[45] The underlying assumption regarding the universe sampled is that it remained homogeneous in all essential factors from 1930 to 1940 for all samples.

[46] For a helpful discussion see Rudolf Carnap, "The Two Concepts of Probability," *Philosophy and Phenomenological Research*, June, 1935, pp. 513–532; Ernst Nagel, "Principles of the Theory of Probability," *International Encyclopedia of Unified Sciences*, vol. 1, No. 6, 1939 (who distinguishes three different meanings of probability—Laplace, Keynes, and Von Mises); and T. C. McCormick, "Note on the Validity of Mathematical Probability in Sociological Research," *American Sociological Review*, October, 1945, pp. 626–631.

[47] and [48] See especially discussions by Carnap and Nagel, *op. cit.*, also our discussion, chap. VII, pp. 183–186.

manner the use of partial correlation technique to analyze relation-ships for the date chosen to show the effect serves as a useful and dependable pre-test of the control factors to use, and saves time and energy that might be expended in trial-and-error attempts to select good controls.

Limitations of the Present Study

Certain qualifications to the present study have been mentioned in passing, but other limitations also require attention. These may be enumerated as follows:

1. In all samples only *the same health areas* of 1940 and 1930 were compared and not the same individuals or families. Only average tuberculosis rates and averages of median rentals for health areas were available and used. This limitation was not present in an earlier study, where the technique of identical individual matching was used to good effect.[49] Matching by statistical devices is effective and yet identical individual matching has the advantage of being simple to comprehend; furthermore, manual manipulation of data in this manner, although more arduous than statistical manipulation, leads to knowing the data more realistically because it is handled.

2. The present study neglects such important variables as: (a) out-migration and (b) in-migration between health areas, since we found no information on these points. This consideration relates to the difficult problem of selective factors discussed below.

3. Only gross rates were computed since data for specific rates by sex, occupation, and other factors were not available.

4. No specific quantitative data of a conclusive type were available on the comparative efficiency of preventive tuberculosis programs in the different health areas. All that is known is that health areas of the experimental group were located in the more crowded central boroughs of the city (Manhattan and Brooklyn), whereas the health areas of the control group were located in outlying boroughs of Bronx and Queens. For nine of the experimental group areas the percentage receiving out of town care, percentage cared for at home, and percentage under care of private physician (presumably those

[49] See pp. 102, 118–119, 123.

receiving superior medical care), were slightly lower than in 16 areas of the control group. This is slender evidence of differential medical care in tuberculosis preventive work.

5. The date periods differ in two cases: for tuberculosis death rates the 1931 figure (used for 1930) is the mean of 1931–1935, and the figure used for 1940 is the mean of 1936–1940. This has the effect of understating the real 1930 rate and of overstating the real 1940 rate, and thus reducing the figure of change from 1930 to 1940.

6. Perhaps the most serious limitation is neglect of the selective factor, which may have operated as follows: high rent areas draw families and individuals of relatively high income, whose economic achievement *may be due* initially to greater physical vigor, stronger physical constitutions, and superior resistance to tuberculosis infection. Low rent areas receive families and individuals whose economic status *may be due* initially to lower physical vigor, weak physical constitutions, and high susceptibility to tuberculosis. This explanation is very different from proving that when a group of families or individuals is moved out of a low rent area into residence in a high rent area, other factors being equal, the tuberculosis death rate of such a moved group declines significantly *following* this move. Our data do not, of course, prove or disprove this proposition. Thus the high rent areas may not operate per se to cause a significant decline in the tuberculosis death rate. The long-time decline in the tuberculosis death rate in the United States since 1900 is no doubt in part a phenomenon of natural selection, the elimination by death of susceptible strains in the population, and the survival of immune strains to form an increasing proportion of the surviving population year after year, until some stable relationship is established for any given stage of development of the arts and sciences. Such an interpretation, however, does not depreciate the valuable contributions made by preventive programs of public health and personal hygiene; nor should it be taken as an argument to weaken the support given to such preventive programs.

As we have seen in Chapter IV, the null hypothesis offers some advantages in the scientific study of the results of applying a social program because it minimizes the bias that can so easily arise in the use of normative terms. The null hypothesis may also be used in experimental studies which attempt to test the effect of impersonal social forces like rentals in the tuberculosis study. Formulated for test by the evidence of this study the null hypotheses would be:

1. There are no changes in tuberculosis death rates and rentals in New York City health areas from 1930 to 1940 when differences in the composition of an experimental and a control group are held constant on two matching factors.

2. The observed changes in tuberculosis death rates and rentals are not greater than those that could occur between two groups selected at random as samples from the same population.

3. The differences in observed changes in tuberculosis death rates and rentals between the experimental group and the control group are not greater than those that could occur between two groups selected at random as samples from the same population.

As we have seen in the discussion of Tables 24, 25, and 26, null hypothesis 1 is disproved. Null hypothesis 2 is disproved for changes in rental for all samples or groups, but supported by the evidence on tuberculosis death rates in the upper quartile group, the experimental group, and the stratified random sample—see Table 25, column (5). Null hypothesis 3 is disproved for rentals, but not for tuberculosis death rates.

Summary Comments

The purpose of observation under conditions of control, as exemplified in the three ex post facto experimental studies just summarized, is to isolate the relationship between one independent variable, assumed to be the chief causal factor or pattern of factors, and a dependent variable, taken as the effect. The operations are simplified by control through matching of several other independent variables known by prior study to be related to the dependent or effect variable.

An appraisal of the comparative success of two of the foregoing experimental tests of the results of a program, those of public housing and public high school education, seems to indicate that a rather simple method of study, like the New Haven experiment, can yield results decisive enough to warrant repetition of the experiment.

The St. Paul study of the effects of high school education on economic adjustment in the community is much more elaborate than the New Haven investigation. For this reason it was possible to analyze the degree of precision with which the several control factors operated singly and in combination. Again, the experimental test of the results of the program was sufficiently decisive to encourage repetition of this form of experimental test.

But the New York City study of rentals and tuberculosis death rates is not comparable to the other two studies despite the fact that in it also the experimental design method was used. As noted on page 136, this study was severely limited by the nature of the units used—health areas and rentals. It may be regarded, therefore, merely as an exploratory investigation to determine the possibility of an application of ex post facto experimental design to the testing of hypotheses about human relations in the ecological frame of reference. Yet even this study yielded sufficiently definite results, in our opinion, to suggest that it may be possible to isolate complexes of cause-and-effect relationships on a physical area basis. The investigations in human ecology have already stimulated an improvement in official recording of many social variables by small physical space areas (census tracts) in American cities. Consequently this study may open up a somewhat novel lead to further research in human ecology. This hope is perhaps the chief justification for including it along with the other two more effective demonstrations of the utility of ex post facto experimental design.

Chapter VI

SOCIOMETRIC SCALES AVAILABLE FOR CONTROL
AND THE MEASUREMENT OF EFFECTS[1]

ALL shrewd observers of human relations, whether as businessmen, nurses, physicians, teachers, or trained social scientists, know that social cause and effect is extremely complex. We live in a veritable web of circumstance. Factors operate functionally so that it is often difficult to decide which is the cause and which the effect. Combinations of many factors in a given social situation still further obscure the real cause-and-effect relationships. But as we have attempted to show in the preceding chapters of this book, some studies have been made by use of experimental designs which open the way at least on the road to systematic and objective observation of human relations, and achieve this result to some degree by control of several of the factors operating in any given social situation. There are, of course, many unknowns still operating and still to be discovered and defined; and only time and continuous research can remedy this limitation. Meanwhile it may be helpful to review briefly a list of instruments of social observation available for use in studies by experimental design.

There are, in general, three groups of variable factors that need to be differentiated in the effort to unravel and observe separately the numerous factors operating in any given social situation: first, there is the dependent variable, the effect we wish to observe and describe; second, there is the independent variable that we have designated as the causal factor, and sometimes this independent variable is itself composed of several interwoven factors operating more or less as a unit pattern; and third, there are other inde-

[1] Part of this chapter was originally published under the title, "Trends in Sociometrics and Critique," by F. Stuart Chapin, in *Sociometry*, July, 1940, pp. 245–262; and in the author's article, "Algunos Metódos Investigación Sociológica en Los Estados Unidos," in *Revista Mexicana De Sociologia*, Enero-Avril, 1944, pp. 19–36.

pendent variables which, if allowed to operate freely, tend to obscure the real relationship between the first two, the relationship we wish to measure by use of experimental design of study. Some of the variables in this third group are known because of previous studies of the same problem; others are unknown.[2]

All three types of factors have to be observed and measured if we hope to explain the relationships, such as housing and juvenile delinquency, counseling and adjustment, or others, which are the problems to be studied.

To be able to observe scientifically, that is, to describe and record objectively what is before us, a large number of instruments of observation are needed. For some variable factors there exist conventional records of the kind or the degree in which different persons possess these factors. Such, for example, are the categories of age, sex, national language, some racial traits, income classes, occupational groups, years of school education, etc. But for many important factors there are no conventional records of kind or degree that can be used as a basis of description. These factors are often psychological, such as morale, personal adjustment, and social distance; they are sometimes obscure community influences which operate by way of gossip, habits of borrowing and lending, or as numerous folkways; and some of them are merely accepted forms of behavior which nobody has thought it important to take down or to keep a record of—and yet some of these, like memberships, attendance, committee assignments, and official positions in the small free groups and organizations of the community, are very reliable and significant indicia of leadership and other highly dynamic social forces. Sociometric scales have been invented in very substantial number, as presently will appear, to permit quantitative description of these factors in human relations.

The remainder of this chapter will be devoted to a description and grouping of these scales of social observation. In this connection no claim is made for the completeness of the list, and readers will

[2] Control of these unknown factors by randomization is difficult to accomplish in the free community situation, as has been noted in earlier chapters of this book, and as will be considered in chap. VII.

doubtless think of excellent scales unfortunately omitted. Our purpose is merely to show the range of observational tools already available for use by the social observer who desires to record his description of the social situation before him in an objective manner. Objective records are of utmost importance if we are to avoid the insidious influence of bias and the desire to find that which we wish. Observation of the qualities of human beings in their social relationships should be stated or recorded in terms that *represent* or that *stand for* these qualities, since it is far too easy to allow our observations to take the form of terms which *express* how the observer *feels* about these qualities. Thus the presumably descriptive term "communist" may be applied to a person not because the record shows that he is a member of the Communist party, has paid dues for the past ten years, and has held office for two years, but because we do not like him as a person. An assumedly descriptive word becomes merely an opprobrious term to express our dislike. Even a more objective term such as "moron," originally used to describe a class of individuals whose scores on a standardized intelligence test were within a certain range of magnitude, may become emotionally toned, as when one says, "Oh, he is nothing but a moron after all," thus expressing disgust at this person but by no means describing him. This example illustrates one of the difficulties to calm, dispassionate, and unbiased observation of human relations. We habitually respond to human relations in terms of emotion and sentiment because these relations possess values for us. It is the achievement of psychometric tests and of sociometric scales that these instruments of observation minimize such distortions and supply the student with devices that measure human relationships.

Sociometry or Social Measurement

By the term "measurement" is meant simply description that uses numerical symbols instead of verbal or ordinary word symbols. For example, it is possible to say that John is taller than Bill, thus describing the stature of these two persons by ordinary words. But when we say that John is six feet two inches (6′ 2″), and Bill is five feet two inches (5′ 2″), we have a much more precise and verifiable form of description. For many purposes the ordinary distinction in words that John is taller than Bill suffices. But if we desire more precision, then we have to resort to measurement in feet and inches. Thus measurement is a form of quantitative word description as distinguished from qualitative word description. We make the transition from one to the other whenever a scale of reference is used as the common unit of description. This scale of reference has no inherent rightness or wrongness and possesses no absolute attributes. It has, like other social products, evolved in practice to meet a need. Some measures, like the foot rule, are the pure result of use and wont; others, like the meter stick, have been somewhat more rationally derived. All depend for their validity upon general acceptance, and all are, in a certain sense, arbitrary constants accepted for their convenience. Since we have been writing for some years on the subject of measurement of social phenomena,[3] we shall not labor the point further, except to say that those who protest that there can be no social measurement are, like the medieval Schoolmen, arguing a lost cause, since we now have an abundance of social measurements. The claim that there can be no social measurement is like the scholastic escape from reality into the realm of dialectic, as when the determination of how many teeth a cow had was decided by the number of quotations that the orators could assemble from Aristotle upon this profound subject, rather than by looking into a cow's mouth and counting the teeth. We have looked into the cow's mouth, we have counted the teeth, and we have found that measurement is a good thing.

What was really done when the cow's teeth were counted? Were the teeth measured? The cow's mouth was described by this operation, but the teeth were not actually measured. Suppose in addition to counting the cow's teeth we had taken a pair of small calipers and found the width and height above the gum of each tooth. That would have been true measurement. Why? The distinction is im-

---

[3] F. Stuart Chapin, "The Meaning of Measurement in Sociology," *Publication of the American Sociological Society,* May, 1930, pp. 83–94; and *Contemporary American Institutions,* Harper & Brothers, 1935, or W. C. Brown, 1946, chap. 27, pp. 353–357.

portant but often overlooked. It is this: Counting the cow's teeth merely enumerated the objects to be described. It all depends upon what is counted. *In enumeration we count objects* to be studied or to be described. *In measurement we count the units on a scale* of reference. The number of units on the scale that corresponds to each subject of observation (tooth) is the measurement of that subject (tooth). Perhaps the confusion arises because population count is often a fact of descriptive procedure in sociology. It is sometimes said that when we count the population of some area such as a city or a county we have measured the population of that area. While it is true that such a statement is descriptive of the area, it is not measurement in any rigorous sense. This is a use of the term "measurement" that no psychologist or biometrist would make. It seems that the more rigorous use of the term is less likely to lead to confusion.

Having cleared the ground of some popular confusions in usage of the concept "social measurement," we may now proceed to a classification of the field of social measurements broadly considered. It is useful to mark off three areas of social measurement: first, psychometrics, or psychological measurements, which includes intelligence tests of a verbal or performance character, educational tests and measurements, personality tests and measurements,[4] attitude scales and measurements,[5] and similar measurements of the reactions of individuals as individuals; second, a division of social

[4] C. Schettler, "Topical Summaries of Current Literature: Personality Traits," *American Journal of Sociology,* September, 1939, pp. 234–258. Supplies 308 titles.

[5] D. D. Droba, "Methods for Measuring Attitudes," *Psychology Bulletin,* May, 1932, pp. 309–323. Supplies 125 titles. More recent summaries and scales such as the following are to be noted: Hugh Carter, "Recent American Studies in Attitudes Toward War: A Summary and Evaluation," *American Sociological Review,* June, 1945, pp. 343–351; H. W. Dunham, "Topical Summaries of Current Literature: Social Attitudes," *American Journal of Sociology,* November, 1940, pp. 344–375; "Methods of Personality Study: A Symposium," Department of Sociology, University of Chicago (mimeographed), 1946; E. W. Noland, "An Application of Scaling to an Industrial Problem," *American Sociological Review,* October, 1945, pp. 631–642; Marion Strauss, "The Construction of a Multidimensional Scale to Measure Attitudes toward Labor Unions" (unpublished), M.A. thesis, University of Minnesota, August, 1945; and Hornell Hart, "A Reliable Scale of Value-Judgments," *American Sociological Review,* August, 1945, pp. 473–480.

measurements called "demogrametrics," or measures of large units of population such as a community, a city, or a state; and third, sociometrics proper, which is the chief subject matter of this discussion. Let us now describe in more detail these three areas of social measurement, broadly considered. In so doing, however, we shall attempt merely to indicate the different types of scales that have been developed, for to attempt any complete coverage would run up a total of considerably over 1000 titles of books and articles.

Psychometrics, defined to include educational tests and measurements, personality tests and measurements, and attitude scales, overlaps the area of sociometrics in that both subjects would include the phenomena of individual behavior and individual response in social situations. Consequently we shall pass over psychometrics with the observation that the measurement of attitudes and of some personality traits will be included in our effort to deal with sociometrics.

Demogrametrics, or the measurement of the forms or results of social behavior in large units such as the community, the city, or the state, also overlaps the field of sociometrics proper, but requires somewhat more consideration. Perhaps the earliest systematic effort to measure the comparative standing of large American cities was made by William F. Ogburn[6] and published in 1917, and a more recent systematic effort to measure the quality of living in American cities is that of Edward L. Thorndike.[7] Ogburn's study rated 36 cities on 18 criteria: child labor, church membership, cost of living, death rates, fire loss, illiteracy, infant mortality rates, library books, parks, pavement, population married, public properties, pupils to teacher, school attendance, school property, teachers' salaries, spoken English, and wage rates. Combining the 18 indices, Seattle, Salt Lake City, and Denver stood at the top; and Atlanta, Charleston, S.C., and Birmingham stood at the bottom of the list. Thorndike's recent rating of American cities is a much more elaborate study

[6] William F. Ogburn, "A Statistical Study of American Cities," *Reed College Record,* December, 1917, 41 pp.

[7] E. L. Thorndike, *Your City,* Harcourt, Brace, 1939, and "American Cities and States, Variations and Correlations in Activities, and the Personal Qualities of Residents," *Annals of the New York Academy of Science,* December 22, 1939, pp. 213–298.

using 37 items of comparison in contrast to the 18 used by Ogburn, but the two lists include some common and similar items, although Thorndike extends his analysis to include inter-correlations of many of his items.[8] He draws some large inferences from his analyzed ratings, for example, that P, personal qualities of the population of cities, are more important than I, income, in the determination of G, goodness of a city for good people. Since each of these indices is based upon factual and measured data, it may be said that Thorndike has offered an operational definition of the quality "goodness of life in cities," but here, as in all operational definitions, the definition is as good, or as bad, as the criteria he uses to validate it. Obviously it becomes a question of the degree of acceptance by scientific research students of the criteria. But more of this matter of operationalism later. For the moment, we merely comment upon it in passing.

Another type of rating of cities is provided by the *Appraisal Form for Local Health Work*, published by the Committee on Administrative Practice of the American Public Health Association.[9] Elmer [10] states that the first complete form for field use in rating public health administration was devised by Charles Value Chapin of Providence, R.I., in 1923, and that in 1924 the American Child Health Association constructed a rating schedule to express the results of its survey of health work in 86 cities.

A third type of rating for communities was devised by Nat Frame [11] in 1921. This includes separate and itemized ratings on 47 traits, some of which are matters of fact and some matters of local

[8] E. L. Thorndike, "Variations Among Cities in Per Capita Income," *Journal of the American Statistical Association*, September, 1937, pp. 471–479.

[9] American Public Health Association, 50 West 50th St., New York City, 1st ed., 1938, 185 pp. and "Methods of Making Sanitation Ratings of Milk Sheds," by L. C. Frank, A. W. Fuchs, and W. N. Dashiell, in Reprint no. 1970 from *Public Health Reports*, August 12, 1938, pp. 1386–1399. U. S. Government Printing Office. Since this earlier study, the Committee on Hygiene of Housing of the American Public Health Association has completed an extensive manual which contains devices for the quantitative description of the urban environment: *Standards for Healthful Housing*: vol. I, *Neighborhood Environment of Dwellings*, 1947.

[10] M. C. Elmer, *Social Research*, Prentice-Hall, Inc., 1939, p. 314.

[11] "Lifting the Country," *Extension Division Circular 255*, October, 1921, College of Agriculture, West Virginia University.

opinion, and covers such main categories as: community spirit, citizenship, recreation, health, homes, schools, churches, business, farms, and a summary score to 1000 units, being the cumulative rating on 10 classes of items with a score of 100 points each. Elmer [12] devised a system for rating communities in 1924 on four groups of activities: educational, religious, recreational, and economic. Possibly the first community rating plan that gave special attention to neighborhoods was that of Willis W. Clark and J. Harold Williams [13] published by the Whittier State School (California) in 1919. This scale had five sections: neatness, sanitation, and improvements, first; recreational facilities, second; institutions and establishments, third; social status of residents, fourth; and average quality of homes, fifth. Ratings on a five-point scale were described for each of the five categories. So much for efforts to rate the community, which might be a town, a small city, or a neighborhood.

The fourth type of demographic scale is that which attempts to rate a whole state. Perhaps the most exhaustive example of this effort at measurement is the series of articles in the *American Mercury Magazine,* under the title, "The Worst American State," published in 1931.[14] The first of this series of studies dealt with economics, illiteracy, and newspaper circulation; the second, with medical facts, vital statistics, some religious data, and others; and the third, with the relative standing in wealth, education, health, and the public order.

Of what use are these demographic studies? Can the sociologist use them as tools in scientific research? The fundamental questions are: Do these scales measure social behavior or the results of behavior with a satisfactory degree of reliability; are they valid measures of that which they purport to describe by measurement; and are

---

[12] *Op. cit.,* pp. 295–304.

[13] "A Guide to the Grading of Neighborhoods," publication of the Whittier State School, Bulletin 8, July, 1919.

[14] *American Mercury,* September, 1931, pp. 1–16; October, 1931, pp. 175–188; November, 1931, pp. 355–371. For a more recent study which supplies a basis for rating American states, see G. Hirschfield and C. W. Strow, "Our National Health Program," *American Sociological Review,* February, 1946, pp. 42–52, or Research Council for Economic Security, Chicago, Ill.

they generally accepted among social scientists? An adequate answer would require widespread use of these scales to test them out in order to prove their reliability and their validity. Obviously, only time and use can supply the answer to these fundamental questions. Assuming, however, for the sake of argument, that these scales are reasonably reliable and valid instruments of social observation, we may point out certain ways in which they could be used to advantage. In the first place, they could be used to compare communities in different regions; in the second place, they could be used to measure changes in the same community over a period of years; and in the third place, they could be used to measure social factors that could be equated in control group analysis.[15] By the latter we mean this: Suppose you desire to study the behavior of delinquent boys in two communities. The first thing you need to know is whether the social environment of these two communities is the same; if you had ratings on the two communities on one or more of these scales, you could decide how near alike the two communities were. Or, to state the matter differently, you could select from a list of communities rated in this way those two communities that were nearest alike; having made this selection you would have obtained two communities with a roughly constant social environment and could then proceed to study the relationship between the amount or quality of juvenile delinquency and the operation, let us say, of the juvenile courts.

This brings us to the subject of sociometrics proper. We shall examine briefly two groups of sociometric scales: first, those that attempt to measure the interaction process within social groups, and second, those that attempt to measure the family group and the home environment.

The measurement of interaction within the social group may be further broken down into five sub-types of rating scale. There are first those scales or procedures that attempt to measure informal friendship constellations and seem to get at the latent culture patterns of a group of people. Illustrations of this technique are afforded

[15] See chap. v, pp. 40, 109–124.

in the recent work of Moreno,[16] Lundberg,[17] Loomis,[18] and Franz.[19] In the second place, there have been rating scales and experimental studies that center upon the description and analysis of the informal play groups of children and young persons. Illustrations of this technique are afforded by the work of Parten,[20] Thomas,[21] Arrington,[22] and Newstetter and his co-workers.[23] The third type of measurement of social interaction as embodied in its effects upon social institutions is through the study of formal organizations, and designated by a scale to measure social participation. Here we have in mind our own work on social participation first outlined in 1924[24] and more recently described by results in 1939.[25] The fourth type of effort to measure the interaction process or its results is seen in the various

[16] J. L. Moreno, *Who Shall Survive*, 1934.

[17] G. A. Lundberg and Mary Steele, "Social Attraction-Patterns in a Village," *Sociometry*, January-April, 1938, pp. 375–419.

[18] C. P. Loomis and D. Davidson, Jr., "Sociometrics and the Study of New Rural Communities," *Sociometry*, January, 1939, pp. 56–76; and "Social Relationships and Institutions in Seven New Rural Communities," *Social Research Report*, no. 18, Bureau of Agricultural Economics and U. S. Department of Agriculture, Farm Security Administration, January, 1940.

[19] J. G. Franz, "Survey of Sociometric Techniques," *Sociometry*, October, 1939, pp. 76–92.

[20] Mildred B. Parten, "Social Participation Among Pre-School Children," *Journal of Abnormal and Social Psychology*, October-December, 1932, pp. 243–269; and "Leadership among Pre-School Children," *ibid.*, January-March, 1933, pp. 430–440; and *ibid.*, July-September, 1933, pp. 136–147.

[21] D. S. Thomas, A. M. Loomis, and R. E. Arrington, *Observational Studies of Social Behavior*, vol. 1, *Social Behavior Patterns*, Institute of Human Relations, Yale University, 1933, 271 pp.

[22] *Ibid.*

[23] W. I. Newstetter, J. J. Feldstein, and T. M. Newcomb, *Group Adjustment, A Study in Experimental Sociology*, School of Applied Social Sciences, Western Reserve University, 1938, 154 pp.

[24] F. Stuart Chapin, "Leadership and Group Activity," *Journal of Applied Sociology* (*Sociology and Social Research*), January-February, 1924, pp. 141–145. In this connection also the work of W. A. Anderson, "The Family and Individual Social Participation," *American Sociological Review*, August, 1943, pp. 420 ff., and December, 1943, pp. 721 ff., deserves attention: also "Family Social Participation and Social Status Self-Ratings," *ibid.*, June, 1946, pp. 253–257.

[25] F. Stuart Chapin, "Social Participation and Social Intelligence," *American Sociological Review*, April, 1939, pp. 157–166.

scales to measure social distance by Bogardus in 1925,[26] by Dodd in 1935,[27] by Chapin in 1934,[28] and most recently by Zeleny.[29] Finally, the fifth sub-type of measurement of social interaction or of its effects is illustrated by Williams' scale for the grading of neighborhoods in 1916,[30] and more recently (1933) by the extremely interesting scale by Jessie Bernard[31] to measure neighborhood folkways.

Social interaction is now receiving attention in the new fields of industrial sociology and in occupational sociology by Goodenough,[32] Guttman,[33] Miller,[34] and Noland.[35]

Having elaborated the measurement of interaction within the social group in terms of studies of informal friendship constellations, play groups and informal groups, formal social organizations and social institutions, and social distance and neighborhood groups and institutions, we may again ask the question, as before, To what

[26] E. S. Bogardus, "Measuring Social Distances," *Journal of Applied Sociology* (*Sociology and Social Research*), March-April, 1925, pp. 299–308.

[27] Stuart C. Dodd, "A Social Distance Test in the Near East," *American Journal of Sociology,* September, 1935, pp. 194–204, and "A Test of Group Preferences in the Near East," American University of Beirut, 1933, 4 pp.

[28] F. Stuart Chapin, "Degrees of Kinship Intimacy," *Sociology and Social Research,* November-December, 1934, pp. 117–125; and reprinted as chap. 20 in *Contemporary American Institutions,* Harper & Brothers, 1935.

[29] Zeleny's recent studies explore the concepts of group morale (not individual morale, cf. E. A. Rundquist and R. F. Sletto, *Personality in the Depression,* University of Minnesota Press, 1936) in his "Sociometry of Morale," *American Sociological Review,* December, 1939, pp. 799–808; group leaders, in his "Characteristics of Group Leaders," *Sociology and Social Research,* November-December, 1939, pp. 140–149, and "Objective Selection of Group Leaders," *ibid.,* March-April, 1940, pp. 326–333; and status, in his "Measurement of Social Status," *American Journal of Sociology,* January, 1940, pp. 576–582. In this connection the criticisms of Zeleny's work and rejoinder should be noted in *American Journal of Sociology,* March, 1940, pp. 771–776.

[30] Williams, *op. cit.*

[31] Jessie Bernard, "An Instrument for the Measurement of Neighborhood with Experimental Applications," *Southwestern Social Science Quarterly,* September, 1937.

[32] W. H. Goodenough, "A Technique for Scale Analysis," *Educational and Psychological Measurement,* Autumn, 1944, pp. 179–190.

[33] L. Guttman, "A Basis for Scaling Qualitative Data," *American Sociological Review,* April, 1944, pp. 139–150.

[34] D. C. Miller, "The Social Factors of the Work Situation," *American Sociological Review,* June, 1946, pp. 253–257.

[35] Noland, *op. cit.,* and footnote 5.

uses may these new tools be put by the research sociologist? How can they be used to solve social problems? Queen and Thomas[36] make use of the Jessie Bernard *Neighborhood Scale* in studies of the city and of urban ecology. In studies of slum clearance in Minneapolis in 1935–1936, the present author [37] used the Rundquist-Sletto scales that measure *morale* (individual morale) and *general adjustment*,[38] *social participation* and *social status,* to secure a pattern of social and individual adjustment by slum families, first in the slum neighborhood, and then after eight to ten months' relocation in different residences during slum demolition. Loomis[39] has shown how the Moreno technique of measuring friendship constellations may be used to select families for colonization in Resettlement Administration Projects of the Farm Security Administration. Many of the scales cited have been used in the study of race prejudice.[40]

The second group of sociometric scales to be considered are those that measure the family group and the home as a social environment. Two sub-groupings of these scales may be conveniently made: The first deals with attitudes and interests of members of a family, and the work of Clifford Kirkpatrick [41] may be cited as an illustration of this approach; the second includes some 19 scales devised to measure various aspects of status, defined as socio-economic status or as social status. Since the work of Kirkpatrick in measuring the

[36] S. A. Queen and L. F. Thomas, *The City,* McGraw-Hill, 1939, pp. 100, 308, 370. See also measurement of community satisfactions in E. C. McVoy and Lowry Nelson, *Agricultural Extension Bulletin 370,* University of Minnesota, 1943.

[37] F. Stuart Chapin, "The Effects of Slum Clearance and Rehousing on Family and Community Relationships in Minneapolis," *American Journal of Sociology,* March, 1938, pp. 744–763.

[38] These scales were published in E. A. Rundquist and R. F. Sletto, *Personality in the Depression,* University of Minnesota Press, 1936.

[39] *Op. cit.*

[40] D. Young, *American Minority Peoples,* Harper & Brothers, 1932.

[41] Clifford Kirkpatrick, "The Measurement of Ethical Inconsistency in Marriage," *International Journal of Ethics,* July, 1936, pp. 444–460; "Community of Interest and the Measurement of Marriage Adjustment," *The Family,* June, 1937; and "Content of a Scale for Measuring Attitudes Towards Feminism," *Sociology and Social Research,* July-August, 1936, pp. 512–526; and by his students in M.A. theses as follows: B. Rosenthal, "Standardization of a Community of Interest Scale, as a Measure of Marital Adjustment," June, 1939; and L. Gross, "Construction of a Belief Pattern Scale for Measuring Attitudes toward Romanticism," August, 1939.

attitudinal complex of family life falls in the overlap zone of psychometrics and sociometrics, we merely mention his work in passing,
and turn to a more detailed discussion of the various types of scales
that measure socio-economic status, broadly considered.

Scales that attempt to measure socio-economic status rate on one
feature (occupational class)[42] or upon several features,[43] and may
require a visit to the home to procure the information,[44] or may be
secured without a home visit.[45] Furthermore, in all of these scales,
the economic or material culture features weigh heavily. Sometimes
there are items that include inquiries about occupation, neighborhood (McCormick, Leahy); often there are items that include education, school attendance, books, magazines (McCormick, Leahy,
Sims); and sometimes only one of these items is included, as books
or magazines (Chapin, Morgan-Leahy). In all of them weights are
assigned to the presence of items deemed to be indicative of the level
of status of the family, and penalties, or negative weights, are oc-
casionally given for a few items (Chapin). Some include articles of
furniture or housing conditions (Chapin, Commons). No generalization about the type of items can be made since the range of items
is large. On the other hand, those scales that have been standardized
are commonly the product of systematic research that involves such
familiar and conventional procedures as the determination of their
reliability and validity, and item analysis to secure an objective basis
of the item weights.[46] In regard to the method of scale construction

---

[42] Scales by Taussig (1913), Barr (1918), Kornhauser (1918), and Anderson and
Goodenough (1931).

[43] Burdick (1928), Chapman-Sims (1925), Chapin (1928, 1933, 1936), Commons
(1908), Engel (1895), LePlay (1885), Leahy Shea (1935), Holley (1916), McCormick
(1929), Perry (1913), Williams (1918), Sewell (1939), E. L. Kirkpatrick (1924,
1933), Sydenstricker and King (1917), and Zimmerman (1924).

[44] Scales of Chapin, Commons, Leahy, McCormick, Perry, Williams, Sewell, E. L.
Kirkpatrick, Sydenstricker and King, and Zimmerman.

[45] Scales of Barr, Burdick, Chapman-Sims, Holley, Kornhauser, Sims, and Taussig
do not require a home visit, but may be filled out on interview or in school by any
informed member of the family.

[46] Consult Mary J. McCormick, *A Scale for Measuring Social Adequacy,* October
15, 1930, *Social Science Monographs,* vol. 1, no. 3, National Catholic School of
Social Service, Washington, D.C.; Alice M. Leahy, *The Measurement of Urban Home
Environment,* University of Minnesota Press, 1936; V. M. Sims, *The Measurement*

used, we can generalize to the extent of saying that those scales concerning which coefficients of reliability and coefficients of validity have been published, based upon good samples, are tools of observation that can be used without hesitation in social research. Usually also, the norms of measurements are published. By norms we mean the average scores on a given scale usually found for different age groups, occupational groups, income groups, relief groups, non-relief groups, or slum groups. By reference to these norms the research worker can determine the departures, if any, of the group of subjects he is investigating, from the expected.

To what practical or theoretical uses have these scales been put? They have been used to compare families in slum areas with families in middle-class areas, to compare foster homes with natural homes, to compare one neighborhood of a community with another, and to measure the change in status during depression years.[47] They may be used in experimental studies in the community to control the factor of social status in comparisons before and after rehousing, before and after moving, etc.[48] Since they have been used to measure social status before and after some social action program has been put into operation, they may to this extent be used to measure social adjustment to changed conditions. When several sociometric scales are used simultaneously, in "before" and "after" measurements, they may be used (with limitations) to measure a pattern of social adjustment.[49] From a theoretical point of view, these scales may be used to

---

of *Socio-Economic Status,* Public School Publishing Co., Bloomington, Ill., 1928; F. Stuart Chapin, *Contemporary American Institutions,* Harper & Brothers, 1935, chap. 19, being a reprint of a pamphlet of 1933; and W. H. Sewell, "The Construction and Standardization of a Scale for the Measurement of Farm Family Socio-Economic Status, University of Minnesota Ph.D. thesis, 1939. The most recent standardized scale to measure urban housing is *An Appraisal Method for Measuring the Quality of Housing* (a yardstick for health officers, housing officials, and planners), Part I, "Nature and Uses of the Method," Committee on Hygiene of Housing, American Public Health Association, 71 pp., 1945. For rural housing, see Howard Cottam, *Housing and Attitudes toward Housing in Rural Pennsylvania,* Pennsylvania State College, Bulletin 436, 1942, Agricultural Experiment Station; C. I. Mosier, *Evaluating Rural Housing,* University of Florida Press, Gainesville, Fla.

[47] See chap. iv, footnotes 9, 11, 13.
[48] See chap. iv, pp. 58–79.
[49] See chap. iii, pp. 41–50.

obtain an operational definition of the concept "social status," previously defined only in verbal terms. The same generalization may be made of all other sociometric scales properly standardized. On the whole, the more carefully calibrated scales, that is, those that enable the student to measure finer gradations of any measured trait among a group of subjects, are the attitude scales and the social status scales.[50] The demogrametric scales are still rather crude instruments. In general, one may judge the dependability of any scale by ascertaining whether the standardization procedures, item analysis, reliability coefficients, validity coefficients, and norms have been published.[51] Reliability coefficients should usually be at least $+.80$ and preferably over $+.90$, and should be based upon correlations of first and second ratings on the same subjects by the same or by different raters, rather than on split-half correlation. Validity coefficients are a much more difficult and technical problem, as Bowers[52] and Chapin[53] have shown. Validity coefficients are usually smaller than reliability coefficients, and correlations ranging from $+.40$ to $+.79$ are usually dependable. Validity coefficients as high as $+.90$ are seldom desirable because they can signify that since the criterion scale (validating scale) measures the trait as well as the new scale does, it may have been unnecessary to construct the new scale at all, since the trait has already been measured satisfactorily by an existing scale.

The next steps in the use or application of sociometric tools are: (1) in the operational definition of sociological concepts and (2) as instruments to provide measured controls, or as criteria of effect, in experimental studies.

[50] Descriptions of the social status scales not identified by footnote citation in this article will be found in the monographs cited by Chapin, Leahy, McCormick, and Sims.

[51] For a discussion of some of the recent scales see F. Stuart Chapin, "New Trends in Social Research—Some Hypotheses and Some Sociometric Scales," *Journal of Educational Sociology*, May, 1938, pp. 561–568.

[52] R. V. Bowers, "An Analysis of the Problem of Validity," *American Sociological Review*, February, 1936, pp. 69–74, based upon R. F. Sletto, "A Critical Study of the Criterion of Internal Consistency in Personality Scale Construction," *ibid.*, pp. 61–68.

[53] F. Stuart Chapin, "Definition of Definitions of Concepts," *Social Forces*, December, 1939, pp. 153–160.

Recently there has been considerable discussion about the possibility of applying to the clarification of sociological concepts the operational procedures found so effective in physics. Since there is not time in this brief section to discuss this problem and the growing controversy that surrounds it with any degree of thoroughness, we shall merely call attention in this connection to recent work by Alpert,[54] Blumer,[55] Chapin,[56] Dodd,[57] Lundberg,[58] Merton,[59] and Stevens.[60] Our own point of view can be stated briefly by quoting from a recent article, "Definition of Definitions of Concepts," published in the December, 1939, issue of *Social Forces*. The whole problem clarifies itself when it is recognized that the so-called operational definition is not set up as any final or absolute solution, but merely as a useful development in the direction of objectivity, and needs to be oriented against the background of sociological literature that will always have to rely heavily upon qualitative word definitions.

The problem is this: since the operational definition of a social concept depends upon the series of acts performed by the investigator in the process of measurement, how can one be sure whether the scale of measurement used really does measure the subject or the objects to which it is applied? This is the problem of validity of the scale of measurement. But the operational definition that science holds up as a desired goal of objectivity states that the measurement is the concept.

Let us consider an illustration of this point. In the trend toward quan-

---

[54] H. Alpert, "Operational Definitions in Sociology," *American Sociological Review*, December, 1938, pp. 855–861.

[55] H. Blumer, "The Problem of the Concept in Social Psychology," *American Journal of Sociology*, March, 1940, pp. 707–719.

[56] F. Stuart Chapin, "Definition of Definitions of Concepts," *Social Forces*, December, 1939, pp. 153–160.

[57] Stuart C. Dodd, "A System of Operationally Defined Concepts for Sociology," *American Sociological Review*, October, 1939, pp. 619–634.

[58] G. A. Lundberg, "The Thoughtways of Contemporary Sociology," *American Sociological Review*, October, 1936, pp. 703–723, and "The Measurement of Socioeconomic Status," *ibid.*, February, 1940, pp. 29–39; and *Foundations of Sociology*, Macmillan, 1940.

[59] R. K. Merton, "Fact and Factitiousness in Ethnic Opinionnaires," *American Sociological Review*, February, 1940, pp. 13–28.

[60] S. S. Stevens, "The Operational Basis of Psychology," *American Journal of Psychology*, April, 1935, pp. 323–330, and "The Operational Definition of Psychological Concepts," *Psychology Review*, November, 1935, pp. 517–527.

titative description or measurement in social psychology and sociology, we strive to define each concept in terms of the measurements upon it. Scales to measure public opinion are constructed and tested for validity. We say of a scale that has been standardized to measure public opinion, "Public opinion is what this scale measures." This is then the operational definition of the concept public opinion. Does this statement of operationalism make meaningless or false the basic question of validity, which is "Does this scale measure that which it is designed to measure, namely, public opinion?" This apparent dilemma appears at first glance to be destructive of the very basis of operationalism, because the proposition appears to beg the question by assuming the conclusion which is to be proved and making it part of the premises used to prove it. In reality, however, the dilemma is not a real one, because the assertion, "Public opinion is what this scale measures," is made only *after* the scale has been standardized. The process of standardization, if done thoroughly, disposes of the question of validity, so that the assertion of the operational form of the definition of public opinion does not beg the question.

We come finally to the use of sociometric tools as a means of providing measured controls or objective criteria of effect in experimental studies.

In the use of sociometric tools to obtain measured controls in studies of matched groups, it may be pointed out that if one desires to hold constant the factor of social status in a comparison between families with delinquent boys and families not having delinquent boys in order to eliminate the influence of status on behavior, the procedure is to select for comparison those families with the same scores on social status as measured by one or more of the scales noted in this section. This simple illustration of the principle may be extended to the use of a battery of sociometric scores to control or limit the variability in certain factors so as to be able to observe the relationship between two other free variables whose cause and effect or other relationship we wish to isolate. This procedure is often used in the form of matching an experimental group and a control group on the occupational factor, in order to observe the relationship between two other variables studied, with the occupational factor held constant.

Summary Classification of Sociometric Scales

1. Psychometric Scales: psychological measurements including
   (1) intelligence tests
   (2) personality tests and scales
   (3) attitude tests and scales
2. Demogrametrics: measurement of the forms or results of social behavior in large units such as the community, the city, and the state
   (1) the quality of living in American cities (Ogburn, Thorndike)
   (2) appraisal of local public health (A.P.H.A., and C. V. Chapin)
   (3) rating smaller communities (Frame, Elmer, Williams)
   (4) rating an American state (*American Mercury*, Hirschfield)
3. Sociometric Scales: measurements of the social process
   (1) interaction within the social group
      a. measurement of informal friendship constellations (Moreno, Lundberg, Loomis, Franz)
      b. measurement of informal play groups of children (Parten, Thomas, Loomis, Arrington, and Newstetter)
      c. measurement of activity within formal groups (F. S. Chapin, W. Anderson)
      d. measurement of social distance (Bogardus, Dodd, F. S. Chapin, and Zeleny)
      e. measurement of neighborhood influences and occupations (J. Bernard, Goodenough, Guttman, Miller, and Noland)
   (2) attitudes and interests of members of the family (Kirkpatrick, Gross, etc.)
   (3) social status, socio-economic status, and home environment (older scales by Commons, Engel, LePlay, Taussig, Barr, Kornhauser, Chapman-Sims, Burdick; and newer scales by Anderson and Goodenough, McCormick, Chapin, Sewell, etc.)

An Illustration of an Application of Semantics and Syntactics to the Improvement of Sociometric Tools[61]

Before concluding this discussion of sociometric scales as tools or instruments of social observation, brief consideration may be given

---

[61] This section appeared originally as an article, "The Syntactical Analysis of Sociometric Techniques: Cases in Point," by F. Stuart Chapin in *Sociometry*, May, 1941, pp. 177–183.

to the use of a new language tool, semantics and syntactics, for the criticism of the items in sociometric scales. Since the social scientist obtains instruments of observation (tools of observation) by constructing sociometric scales, and many of these scales consist of linguistic items rather than of material substances (like the instruments of precise observation of physical science), the student who constructs a new scale must utilize language items with great care. Furthermore, since much social behavior consists of language behavior, vocalization, writing, and linguistic habits of response, complications easily occur when the language behavior of the student (as social scientist) is used to describe and record the language behavior of the subject, the person behaving. Thus we have before us the problem of how to use the tool of language to create a tool of observation to be used in the study of linguistic behavior. In semantics and syntactics we have a key to this problem.

Syntactical analysis is a powerful tool for the dissection of theoretical statements and working hypotheses of social research. This section will examine two cases: first, an assertion about attitude measurement that represents a fairly common philosophic point of view; second, one aspect of the controversy over units of measurement. It is hoped that this brief analysis will clarify some aspects of method. Clarification of method is useful when it furnishes reliable and valid tools or procedures that many other research workers can use with confidence. Such a discussion is not an escape from reality into the petty refinements of technique when specific facts are used to test the points clarified and when those who read the results are left to make their own inferences as to validity and utility.

A Case in the Measurement of Attitude

A statement in the authentic language of social science by a well-known author about attitude measurement is, "They seek to apply *mechanical methods* of measurement to things whose *very nature* they fail to understand" [62] (italics ours).

Analysis of this statement shows that two words, "mechanical methods," function in this sentence with invidious purpose. They

---

[62] Robert M. MacIver, *Society: Its Structure and Changes,* 1931, p. 45.

are a familiar stereotype used in terms of reproof. Second, the statement also uses the other words, "very nature," to imply a metaphysical presupposition. Stereotypes and metaphysical terms are permissible in ordinary language behavior (the folk language) as *subject matter of study,* but are not permissible in the language of science used as *a tool* to describe or to analyze ordinary language behavior. Hence this sentence is what Carnap would call a sentence in the pseudo-thing language and is non-sense. By contrast, the thing sentence that this MacIver statement could be *reduced* to in order to make it have sense, in the empirical science meaning, would be: "They seek to explain attitudes by measurements on scales of such grossness of calibration that the instrument misses differences that may be highly significant."

Probably MacIver would agree that this was what he really meant. He did not, however, state his criticism in this way, but used the all-too-familiar pattern of philosophic language in a context in which an empirical science statement would be expected. We make this last assertion because the original statement is not capable of proof or disproof, whereas the statement in its reduced form is capable of proof or disproof. If the scale in question differentiates between individuals, the proposition is disproved. That such proof can be demonstrated is shown in the analysis of item 47 from the Rundquist-Sletto [63] scale of opinions where relief clients have a 44-per-cent more radical scale position than employed persons.

In item 47 note the use of the word "ought" (italics ours). This word does not make any further statement or assertion about the matter, but is merely equivalent to saying, "The government guarantees a living wage to those who can't work" in a tone of approval or with greater emphasis. The word "ought" is thus merely a word that functions in the sentence to express emotion. The use of this word makes the statement a normative statement incapable of proof, and therefore a pseudo-thing sentence. The word "ought" serves as a normative or ethical symbol, the function of which is emotive, to express emotion or to elicit an emotional response in the subject

---

[63] E. A. Rundquist and R. F. Sletto, *Personality in the Depression,* pp. 384–391, and 394–398.

(the person who responds to the test); as such it is a good statement in the folk language because it is a stimulus to which different degrees of emotional response can be recorded by setting the symbols: $5 =$ strongly agree, $4 =$ agree, $3 =$ undecided, $2 =$ disagree, and $1 =$ strongly disagree. Thus the number symbols stand for or represent different degrees of emotion elicited by the stimulus, and these numerical symbols are susceptible of arithmetic and statistical manipulation to obtain averages for a group.[64]

Sentences from the folk language	"47. The government *ought* to guarantee a living to those who can't find work."	"29. Poverty is a result of *injustice* in the distribution of wealth."

The language of science used as a tool to describe behavior in the folk language	5 4 3 2 1
	
	 Mean scores (1)
	 2.72 Employed
	     (2)
	 3.24 Unemployed
	     (3)
	 3.94 Relief
	 1.22 Differences
		5 4 3 2 1
		
		 Mean scores
		 2.89
		
		 3.14
		
		 3.54
		 0.65

Item 29, in which the stereotype "injustice" (italics ours) serves in an emotive function, is not as effective in differentiating between employed and relief groups as is item 47. Nevertheless both items have critical ratios of over 2, and number 47 is statistically significant. To return to our former point, we may now assert that we have proved that item 47 does not miss differences that are significant, and that therefore this item has a fineness of calibration that distinguishes between the attitudes of employed and relief persons, two groups that would be expected to have different attitudes on this issue. We have thus disproved the statement about attitude measurement when rendered in its *reduced* form, a demonstration

---

[64] This problem has been recently explored under the concept "the intensity function" in attitude research by Guttman, Goodenough, and Noland, *op. cit.*

that could never have been made in the case of the original state-ment in its philosophic phraseology. Hence the value of syntactical analysis applied to the dissection of a loose statement.

Equal and Interchangeable Units of a Scale

Our second case concerns the controversy over units of measure-ments in psychometric and sociometric scales. The proposition that these units are equal and interchangeable has been claimed and de-nied by Kirkpatrick, Merton, J. Bernard, and Lundberg.[65]

This controversy arises for two reasons: first, because of the ab-sence of a clear distinction between (a) units of subject matter or objects of study, which we have designated "units of observation";[66] and (b) units of reference which are arbitrarily assumed equal for purposes of convenience in linear continuum, which we have previ-ously designated "units of measurement."

The controversy arises in the second place because the foregoing distinction between units of observation and units of measurement is difficult to grasp when applied to intangible social attitudes.

Let us begin with the first reason for the controversy. Units of ob-servation, (a), may be similar but can never be equal or interchange-able (one human being[67] is more like another than is any human being like an elephant). On the other hand, units of measurement, (b), on an assumed linear scale are equal and interchangeable distances or numerical weights representing these distances. These units of distance or weights *are arbitrarily set as equal* to assumed degrees of approval or disapproval in attitude measurement. The only way to justify such an assumption is by *using* a scale in which such units are a part of the continuum, and then *finding* that such

[65] Clifford Kirkpatrick, "Assumptions and Methods in Attitude Measurement," *American Sociological Review,* February, 1936; Robert K. Merton, "Fact and Facti-tiousness in Ethnic Opinionnaires," *ibid.,* February, 1940, pp. 13–28; J. Bernard, *ibid.,* June, 1940; G. A. Lundberg, *ibid.,* February, 1940, pp. 38–39; and R. K. Mer-ton, *ibid.,* August, 1940.

[66] F. Stuart Chapin, "The Meaning of Measurement in Sociology," *Publication of the American Sociological Society,* May, 1930, pp. 83–94 (especially pp. 89–92).

[67] It is customary to count the number of persons in two different areas and take the resulting sums as measures of population. This use of the concept measure-ment is loose, as we have pointed out in previous analyses of the concept.

a scale does in fact differentiate by significantly different scores between two groups that are recognized as different on some other accepted device of differentiation. For example, when the Rundquist-Sletto scale shows a mean score of relief persons of 3.94 on item 47, and a mean score of 2.72 for employed persons, the difference, 1.22, is so large as to be scarcely due to pure chance (as understood by reasonable persons). Furthermore, one knows that employed persons and relief clients are in different social situations in terms of economic security. Hence whatever the crudities of the original assumption of linear units, *the scale does work* as a differentiating device. As long as it works it is a useful instrument.

Since the distinction between (a) units of observation and (b) units of measurement is especially difficult to grasp when applied to such intangible things as social attitudes, the arguments pro and con are not easy to substantiate in terms sufficiently concrete to be convincing. We shall next consider, therefore, an example in which the units of observation are not abstractions like social attitudes, but tangible sense data. Take the case of measurements with our social status scale.

Louis Guttman[68] recently completed a multiple factor analysis of the social status scale measurements on 67 Negro families in Minneapolis and St. Paul made in 1932, to test the validity of the numerical weights used in the 1932–1933 edition of the scale.[69] In this scale, which lists articles of furnishings in an ordinary living room, there are 17 items. To explain concretely the distinction between units of observation and units of measurement let us take as examples item 15, newspapers, to which a weight of 8 is assigned, and item 17, radio, to which a weight of 8 is also assigned. The question is, was a weight of 8 the correct weight of each such item if the scale is to

[68] For an abstract of the results of this WPA factor analysis study under the direction of Mr. Guttman see footnote 15, chap. v. It may be stated that this analysis involved the computation of 4305 correlations over a period of more than a year and a half.

[69] F. Stuart Chapin, *Contemporary American Institutions*, Harper & Brothers, 1935, W. C. Brown, 1946, pp. 378–382. In addition to the 17 items of sense data, there are 4 items of opinion, but these items also have satisfactory reliability and validity as tests show, and hence do not affect the argument given herein.

differentiate on total score of the living room between families of different income class, different occupational group, differences in total years of formal education of the parents, and differences in the participation scores[70] of the parents in organized groups of the community?

Guttman shows by factor analysis that new (more valid) weights in comparison with the old (arbitrary) weights may be derived. For instance:

Units	Old Weight	New Weight
4. Fireplace with 3 or more utensils	8	34.6
15. Newspapers (each)	8	7.7
16. Telephone	8	24.4
17. Radio	8	8.0

It is evident from inspection of these four items: (1) that the original weights of items 4 and 16 were quite inaccurate and far too low, and (2) that the original weights of items 15 and 17 were about correct.

What is the bearing of this finding upon the issue of "equal and interchangeable units"? It is this: Factor analysis reveals that the presence of a fireplace and 3 or more utensils (number 4), and the presence of a telephone (number 16), are more significant indicators of differences in social status on four other indices of social status (income, occupation, education, and participation), than we had originally assumed. But factor analysis also proves that weights of 8 each for newspapers and radio were valid weights.[71]

In this example it seems that the objects "newspaper" and "radio" are, when translated into numerical weights, equal and interchangeable units in two meanings: (1) as units of observation, subjects of study to which sensory reactions are made, and also (2) as units of

[70] F. Stuart Chapin, "Social Participation and Social Intelligence," *American Sociological Review*, April, 1939, pp. 157–166.

[71] Further verification of the new Guttman weights is obtained by using them against the old weights in computing a critical ratio between an experimental group of public housing residents and a matched group of slum families for differences in gains on social status from 1939 to 1940, where the critical ratio was increased from 0.8 to 1.77.

measurement, equal and interchangeable numerical weights or distances on an assumed linear scale. The same statement cannot, however, be made of item 4 and item 16, since by Guttman's analysis the importance of the former is 1.4 times the importance of the latter, if we accept the description of social status on the combined evidence of income, occupation, education, and social participation as an external criterion of social status. Thus although two of the items (objects) are of about equal importance numerically, the other two items are not of equal importance numerically. This indicates that in one simple scale at least, *there is no necessary intrinsic correspondence between the weights* (*units of measurement*) *and the objects or subject matter* (*units of observation*). It is purely coincidence that two of the items (newspapers and radio) should turn out to have the same numerical values in the two validations of the scale against external criteria. This analysis does, it seems to us, help clarify the basis of the controversy over the condition that units are equal and interchangeable. Incidentally, it seems to provide evidence in support of our original position of 1930, when the distinction in regard to social measurements was first made, that (1) units of observation (subject phenomena) are not to be confused with (2) units of measurement (reference phenomena), if social measurement as a useful device is to progress to a more precise form of scientific description.

Chapter VII

SOME FUNDAMENTAL PROBLEMS AND LIMITATIONS TO STUDY BY EXPERIMENTAL DESIGNS

In the preceding chapters we have noted the fact that there are many unsolved problems and some fundamental limitations to be overcome in studies by experimental design. Systematic consideration of these difficulties has been deferred for analysis in this concluding chapter. These problems and limitations are of two kinds: first, practical obstacles; and second, theoretical limitations that derive from the conditions of the probability theory wherever critical ratios are used as a provisional test of the statistical significance of differences in means, changes in means, or differences in changes in means of such non-random samples as an experimental group and a control group. We shall now consider the practical obstacles, and then pass to a consideration of the theoretical limitations.

Practical Obstacles[1]

Field interviews of individuals in their homes and in the community setting reveal problems not present in experimental designs that are set up in the comparatively simple schoolroom situation,[2] familiar in educational research. The problems of field interview emerging in the community situation in which research uses some experimental design are both methodological and practical. In this section we shall attempt to describe these problems as they arose in three research studies using three different variations of experi-

[1] This section appeared originally in an article, "Some Problems in Field Interviews When Using the Control Group Technique in Studies in the Community," by F. Stuart Chapin, *American Sociological Review*, February, 1940, pp. 63–68.

[2] E. F. Lindquist, *Statistical Analysis in Educational Research*, Houghton Mifflin, 1940, pp. 80–84.

mental design. Wherever possible, solutions of these problems will be indicated.

To clarify our analyses it should be stated at the outset that by problems of field interview we mean problems of organization and timing of these interviews and not problems of minute personal relationship in interview situations. Since some study has been made of problems that arise in face-to-face contacts of interviewing,[3] and less attention has been given to problems of organization and timing, it is with these latter problems that we shall be concerned, and more specifically with scheduling interviews in home calls chiefly as related to sampling.

The purpose of experimental designs applied to the study of social factors is to measure the effect of one social factor at a time, all other factors in the situation (unknown as well as known) being held constant, that is, controlled. Difficulties arise at once because it is seldom possible to measure one factor alone. Usually the best that we can do is to try to measure a group of factors which operate as social treatment, or as a social program—as, for instance, in an effort to isolate and measure the effect of improved housing upon a group of families formerly slum residents.[4] A second difficulty arises because there are unknown factors at work, that is, unmeasured factors which are not controlled.

Randomization[5] is theoretically the solution to obtaining control of these unknown factors. The procedure is to select a sample at random from the population to be studied. This sample may then be divided at random into the experimental group, which is to receive the social program (e.g., good housing), and the control group, which is excluded from the program (e.g., the slum dwellers). Or two random samples are selected, one to receive the program, the

[3] Twila E. Neely, *A Study of Error in the Interview*, Columbia University Press, 1937; see also several recent studies in *Sociometry*, May, 1942, pp. 109–134. See also R. K. Merton and Patricia L. Kendall, "The Focused Interview," *American Journal of Sociology*, May, 1946, pp. 541–557.

[4] See chap. IV, pp. 58–79.

[5] Lindquist, *op. cit.*, pp. 24–29; T. C. McCormick, *Elementary Social Statistics*, McGraw-Hill, 1941, pp. 27–28; Quinn McNemar, "Sampling in Psychological Research," *Psychology Bulletin*, June, 1940, pp. 331–335, 353.

other to act as a control and to be excluded from the program. Since each random sample is by definition selected without bias it will probably contain the unknown or unmeasured factors in equal degree.

The next step is to measure simultaneously each group on some criteria designed to evaluate the effect of the program (e.g., scales that measure morale, adjustment, social status, social participation, etc.). After an interval of a year or more, each group is again measured. Then if the difference in measured changes between the experimental group and the control group shows that the experimental group gains in a degree that occurs very infrequently in chance, the odds are in favor of concluding that we have discovered a difference that is probably a measure of the effect of the social program.[6] So runs the argument.

In community research in practice, however, we encounter an initial difficulty to this apparently smooth logical conclusion. Some cases disappear during the interval of time that the experiment runs. Some are lost by refusals to give information on second interview, some have become deceased, and some have moved away and cannot be found. As a consequence the terminal groups are not composed of the same individuals as at the outset. This means that at the terminal date the groups have lost their random character. Certain selective influences have been at work.

A possible solution of this dilemma is to select several random samples for experimental groups and several for control groups, on the assumption that at least one pair of samples will not lose cases and hence will remain random samples throughout the experiment. The practical difficulty to be overcome by this remedy is that of cost. When several samples or pairs of samples are used it is necessary to interview many more cases and this procedure rapidly runs up the expense of research. It increases the cost also because a larger number of interviewers have to be trained and supervised.[7]

---

[6] Disproof of null hypotheses is assumed as part of the procedure.

[7] In the housing study cited, the interviews required from 35 to 50 minutes each to fill in the three schedules or scales used, from which the four measures were derived. For a sample of 120 cases, 6 interviews a day would require 20 days, and 10 interviews a day, 12 days.

More serious than this difficulty is another very practical and fundamental one. It is this. Will the directors of a social program be willing to give their treatment to a randomly selected group and exclude from treatment another identical group to provide a theoretically sound experimental design? When we were asked to study the effects upon the morale of clients resulting from a WPA program in comparison to that of general relief (local relief), it was not possible to use a procedure of this sort.[8] Who ever heard of a director of WPA or of relief or of public housing willing to court the public criticism that would develop if it became known that selection for treatment or exclusion was made on a random basis? In the WPA study a public controversy was already under way relative to the continuance or limitation of the program. The public atmosphere was therefore not conducive to strengthening support for a research procedure which seemed to favor certain individuals at the expense of others. People resent being chosen to serve as "guinea pigs." Would a government administrator permit admission to a public housing project of some families and exclusion of others equally eligible on the basis of random choice? Most administrators are charged with the responsibility to admit to good housing only the most needy families, other factors being equal. This is the way social reform programs are set up to function because those who sponsor them never question their beneficial effects any more than they ever expect to bring such programs to a scientific test of their effects. In the housing experiment cited, there had been much criticism of the project from conservative groups of the community and this created for the administrators many practical difficulties. No public administrator would like to be in the position of seeming to favor one group (in this case the experimental group to be selected at random to have the benefit of treatment) at the expense of another group (in this case the excluded control group, also to be selected at random), without tangible evidence of the greater eligibility on the part of the beneficiaries of the program. Once greater eligibility is accepted as a criterion of admission, the randomness of the group disappears,

[8] See chap. III, pp. 41–50.

and with it one of the essential conditions of an ideally theoretical experiment.

Until public administrators of social programs can see their way around this problem, it appears that the use of randomization as a method of control of unknown factors can be ruled out in experimental designs as a method of evaluating social programs in the community situation.

The research student turns, therefore, to the control group technique. This method limits the use of randomization to the selection of the control group. We are obliged to accept as the experimental group any accessible portion of the population eligible to and receiving the program, whether a WPA, relief, or housing program. The control group consists of a random sample selected from a similar population not receiving the program. This was the plan followed in the WPA study cited. In the housing study, for reasons of time limitation placed upon the research, it was not possible to select the control group at random. In this case the control group, like the experimental group, consisted of accessible families living in the slum in the same residence for the duration of the experiment.

To reduce variation among other factors the two groups are then matched on as many known factors as possible. These may be age, sex, size of family, income, occupational class, etc. The experiment proceeds from this point as before: measurements are made before and after on selected criteria of effect. Since individual cases are lost during the interval of the experiment, it is important to ask, "What are the reasons for these eliminations?"

Our experience in two studies using before and after measurements on both an experimental and a control group shows that the longer the experiment runs in a free community situation, the larger the number of cases lost. The first of these two studies was an ex post facto experiment.[9] The purpose of this study was to measure the effect on individual adjustment to community life of the factor, "length of high school education," on the hypothesis that the longer the term of high school education the better the adjustment to com-

9 See chap. v, pp. 99–124.

munity life nine years after graduation or leaving school. We shall not repeat here a full account of this research, since it has been described in Chapter V. The study began with the school records of 2127 St. Paul high school students of 1926. Of these, 1130 had graduated in 1926 after a four-year course, and 997 had in 1926 dropped out of school, in which year they had completed the first, or second, or third year. By 1935, or nine years later, an interview follow-up in the community situation of these 2127 young people found only 1194 cases. During the nine-year interval between leaving school in 1926 and the year 1935, when field interviews began, some 933 of the original 2127, or 43.8 per cent, were lost for further study. The reasons for these losses were: 575 could not be found, 42 had moved out of the community, 21 were deceased, and for 295 the records were so incomplete as to prevent using these cases in further comparative study. Of the experimental group of 1130 graduates in 1926, some 459, or 40.6 per cent, were among those lost for the reasons stated above. Of the control group of 997 school drops or incomplete, 474, or 47.5 per cent, were lost. In this instance, as in other similar studies, the losses were greater from the control group than from the experimental group.

In the second study, the housing study mentioned above, we began with measures of morale, general adjustment, social status, and social participation in 1939, on 108 families admitted to Sumner Field Homes of Minneapolis, and a control group of 131 similar families living in the slum. A total of 48 families were lost before 1940 when the experimental period ended. Of this number, 7 dropped out of the experimental group because they could not be located and 41 were eliminated from the control group. The breakdown of these 41 dropped cases was: 30 not located after careful field work follow-up, 5 moved out of town, and 6 moved into the housing project (hence had to be excluded from the control group). In all, 20 per cent of the initial number of families were lost during the experimental period of one year.

But analysis of the drops due to mobility and miscellaneous reasons does not tell the whole story. In the housing study additional cases were lost owing to refusals to give information after repeated and courteous attempts at interviews. A total of 20 cases were lost for this reason: 6 from the experimental group of residents and 14 from the control group of slum families. Additional miscellaneous reasons accounted for a loss of 7 cases from the control group. In summary, a total of 75 cases were lost [10] in these ways from the 239 original total of both groups. (See Chapter IV, pp. 58–79.) This suggests the degree to which samples would have been distorted from representativeness had it been possible to select the individuals at random. The original samples were not chosen randomly because, as explained above, a social program conducted in the milieu of the contemporary community folkways and mores cannot be applied to random groups of the population. The regulations that express the purpose of such a program require that it be directed to the most needy.

The original experimental group consisted of 108 families that moved into residence in Sumner Field Homes during the period December 15, 1938, to April 15, 1939. They were first interviewed between February 1 and April 15, 1939, and re-interviewed in 1940 from February 1 to May 31. This spread of dates over which the interviews took place illustrates another problem of field work in the community situation. A zero or dead-line date at which all subjects are interviewed usually cannot be set in studies of this kind. Furthermore, the control group too, consisting of 131 families who were rejected applicants to the project, were interviewed over the periods February 5 to July 31 in 1939 and February 15 to April 30 in 1940. As we have noted above, interviewing a control group involves more difficulties than interviewing an experimental group, because individuals in the latter tend to be more receptive to inquiries, whereas more resistance is encountered in the former.

How can the student bring order out of this apparent confusion of factors that present practical problems in studies made in the complicated community situation? The answer is to match the experimental group against the control group on as many known factors as pos-

---

[10] In the WPA study cited above, in which no time interval between measurements made before and after intruded, losses of cases comparable in size and for similar reasons were experienced. See chap. III, pp. 41–50.

sible. But matching causes additional loss of cases which cannot be matched. Thus in the housing study 82 cases were eliminated for this reason: 51 from the experimental group of residents and 31 from the control group of slum families. As the number of matching factors is increased the elimination of cases grows. Thus with 5 matching factors, race or culture class of husband, employment situation of husband, occupational class of husband, number of persons in the family, and income of family, some 47 cases were lost from the experimental group and 10 from the control. When 5 added controls or matching factors were introduced, 4 more dropped out of the experimental group and 21 from the control. Thus the total losses of cases from the original 239 families were for all causes 157 cases, leaving 82 terminal cases that were matched on 10 factors, of which total, 44 cases were in the experimental group and 38 cases in the control group. The total loss was 65.6 per cent for the one-year period of the experiment.

Matching on individuals so that for each individual in the experimental group there is another in the control group alike in respect to score on every one of the matching factors results in very great losses because of inability to satisfy such a precise matching requirement. In the Christiansen experiment this rigorous manual matching procedure diminished the experimental group from 671 to 23 individuals, and the control group from 523 to 23 individuals. In the housing study this method of identical individual matching was not used; matching was by sub-categories. This latter method proceeds by elimination only of cases from one group which are entirely outside the categories of the other group, and is essentially that of insuring comparable frequencies in sub-categories. This method has the great advantage of avoiding numerous losses due to matching. Louis Guttman in his study, "On Uses of the Critical Ratio—A Research Paper," University of Minnesota, June, 1939, pp. 34, 36, has worked out the formulas used.

The next question that arises is, What sort of individuals are lost during the interval that the experiment runs? Are those who drop out because they refuse information on second interview or have moved away different in any respects as a group from those who remain in the samples that carry through the experiment? Are those dropped for reasons of mobility and refusal different types of cases from those lost because of failure to match on factors of control?

Since we had initial measurements in 1939 on morale, general adjustment, social status, and social participation for all cases, we may examine the scores of the dropped cases for comparison with the scores of those that survived to the terminal dates of 1940. It is possible that a systematic recapture program such as used in the study of consumer purchases [11] would have diminished these losses and interpolated the measurements on some missing cases, but it would have considerably changed the dates and places of interview so that measurements on the attitude factors might have been invalidated for purposes of comparison. That is, while changes in date of interview by a few weeks probably did not affect the validity of information on schedules of the study of consumer purchases and on social participation and social status in the housing study, it might have seriously changed an attitude response measured by the *Survey of Opinion* schedule in the housing study. Consequently the time factor in extending the span of time over which field work interviews are made requires careful consideration before a recapture program is organized.

In general, we found that the cases dropped, either by losses or from inability to match on control factors, were cases showing more extreme measurements, that is, higher or lower scores on all scales used to measure the effect (morale, general adjustment, social participation, and social status). Thus the net effect of losses was to increase the homogeneity of the residual groups (experimental and control) from which the results of the experiment were inferred. As a consequence of these facts the magnitude of absolute scale differences between the experimental and the control groups upon measures of effect was small and hence the critical ratios were

[11] Erika H. Schoenberg and Mildred Parten, "Methods and Problems of Sampling Presented by the Urban Study of Consumer Purchases," *Journal of the American Statistical Association*, June, 1937, pp. 311–322.

diminished from this fact alone. Also the reduced size of the residual groups yielded larger standard errors, which, in turn, played a part in still further reducing the size of the critical ratios.

An opportunity presented itself for a check-up in November, 1942, on the original experimental group of residents. The FPHA visitors re-interviewed the families and found only 21 of the original 44 families of the experimental group still residents of the housing project. These third interviews secured 1942 measures on morale, general adjustment, social participation, and social status. On attitude measurements (morale and general adjustment) the 21 families showed decided improvement over their responses in 1939 and in 1940. Whether these gains may be attributed to the effects of living in the housing project or form part of the general improvement of the times we are unable to state. We did find, however, that the remainder of the original experimental group, that had moved away from Sumner Field Homes between 1940 and 1942, showed a somewhat better morale and general adjustment in 1939 and 1940 than did the group of 21 families we were able to follow up in 1942, and who then showed such decided gains.

It will be noted that this 1942 follow-up of resident families revealed a loss of nearly 50 per cent from the original 44 families of 1939–1940. This is the most significant aspect of the follow-up considered in terms of sampling. It shows how difficult it is to preserve the conditions of an experiment for even as few as three years (e.g., 1939 to 1942). If effects of social treatment are to be measured as part of rational programs for evaluating social action, how long does the experiment need to run? If a long time is desired or needed to test the effects of social treatment, then the evidence of this follow-up shows how difficult it may be to complete adequately planned experiments which are to be performed in a free community situation.

We may now tentatively summarize the problems of field interview as found in three community studies using the control group technique in a free community situation.

1. The longer the time of each interview (every additional scale or questionnaire to be filled in extends the time of each interview),

the fewer the cases that can be canvassed with a given size of field staff in a given time.

2. The longer the period (in days or weeks) over which the interviews run, the greater the likelihood that administrative changes will occur and disrupt the conditions of the experiment.

3. The longer the time interval over which the experiment runs, the greater the loss of cases due to mobility and refusals.

4. Such losses are likely to be more numerous in the control group than in the experimental group.

5. The larger the number of factors used in matching, the greater the number of cases that will be dropped.

6. The cases lost by mobility, refusals, matching, etc., tend on the average to be cases with extreme measurements on criteria of effect. Consequently the trend is toward increasing homogeneity in the experimental and the control groups with resulting diminution in magnitude of differences found on measures of effect. This is to say that losses of cases between "before" and "after" measurements tend to leave in the residual groups individuals more alike than was the case at the outset.[12]

In addition to the last point it needs to be recognized that the forms of social treatment which experimental designs attempt to evaluate are usually directed upon populations originally quite homogeneous. To be specific, the kind of people who receive WPA, relief, or public housing programs are people at a relatively low and uniform level of income, occupational class, and educational attainment when the experiment begins. To this fact of original homogeneity are added the effects of losses of cases, which, as shown above, tend to create still further homogeneity. Consequently if any changes have occurred it becomes evident that these can be

[12] The Hill experiment (see chap. IV, pp. 79–84) confirmed some of these problems. But the problem of selection is often present. In the housing study described in the same chapter, the conditions of eligibility for admission to the project obtained among the applicants. Yet these very conditions of low income, family size, ages of children, etc., made both the accepted and the deferred rejected applicants much alike. Thus in so far as inference in this study is confined to the closed system of this single experiment, the invalidating influence of selective factors is disposed of. Confirmation of results in similar experiments is, however, still much to be desired.

described only when the scales that measure effects are sensitive to small differences. Two ways in which such scales may be provided are: (a) to improve existing sociometric scales within their middle ranges by finer calibrations, or (b) to utilize the evidence of several minor changes in the same direction by means of computing multiple critical ratios. This latter procedure enables the research student to measure a pattern of change in several factors.

If cost precludes the use of many samples or the use of larger samples to offset the handicaps inherent in samples attenuated from community influences, it would seem that the two procedures just noted may still supply a partial solution of both the methodological and the practical obstacles to using experimental designs which we have enumerated in this book.

Finally, interference with randomization due to practical considerations of an administrative nature does not by any means invalidate the use of experimental designs in the community situation because the results do hold for the groups studied and within the limits of the known controls. The next step is to repeat the experiment on similar groups under like conditions and when possible with additional or more significant controls. The cumulative findings of several similar experiments may prove to be as useful as would fewer experiments based on control of unknowns by randomization within the sub-groups of a stratified sample.

Theoretical Limitations

Throughout this discussion of experimental designs in sociological research we have frequently used the term statistical significance as a criterion of when a difference between the means of an experimental group and a control group is important, or when a change between the means of observations at two dates is important. Let us now review the meanings of these terms "important" and "significant."

When Is a Difference Significant?

In the folk language a difference is important or not important. It is important if an expert says it is. But the public's judgment of who is an "expert" is often not reliable since there is little common knowledge of technical specialization in science. Consequently importance becomes a matter of opinion. The opinion of interested parties is often taken as a criterion of when a difference between wage rates, a difference in educational achievement, or a difference in need of social treatment is important. In social programs the interested party whose opinion is taken as a criterion of the importance of observed differences is sometimes the promoter.[13] But his opinion of the results of a program is naturally influenced by his *desire* to achieve some end-in-view. Again, it may be the administrator of the program whose opinion of its results is taken as a criterion. But it should be remembered that the administrator has accountability and responsibility for seeing that the end-in-view *is* achieved. Both promoter and administrator are tempted when making a judgment of the importance of a gain associated with a social program to substitute the psychology of *vindication* for the psychology of *verification;* to substitute the notion of justification of a position taken in advance and expressed by emotional appeal *for the operation of confirming the results* of applying a program *by repetition* of the program under like conditions. Thus is the spirit of vindication unconsciously substituted for the spirit of verification. Moreover, these opinions of what is important, or when a difference or a change associated with a program is important, are rendered *after* the experiment is terminated. The results are then value-judgments with an underlying means-ends schema that may be only implicit, and the whole process is subjective.

To be sharply contrasted with the foregoing criterion of significance is the criterion of statistical significance, which is based on differences or changes in the magnitude of measurements. In experimental designs reliance is usually placed on the means of measurements for the sake of comparison with the means of random samples. Now it may be noted that the means are derived from measurements obtained from applying some psychometric or sociometric scale. Furthermore the scale is a reliable instrument of

[13] See pp. 168–169; also chap. IV, p. 78, footnote 22.

observation which has been pre-tested for reliability before use in the study under consideration. It is *reliable* because repeated measurements by the same observer on the same or similar subjects are essentially in agreement; they show small errors of observation. It is perhaps also reliable because measurements independently made by different observers on the same subject agree. The scale is also *valid*. It does measure that which it is designed to measure. There is, first, an initial validation by the selection of items to be included when specialists are asked for judgments upon these items; and there is, second, a terminal validation when the scale is shown to be consistent in discriminating differences equally well with some other scale or external and independent criterion acceptable to research specialists. All these tests are met *before* the scale is used in experimental designs. Moreover, the scale is supplemented by empirical norms,[14] or mean scores derived from its use and differentiating the two groups, so that comparisons can be made, and any new group can be placed with reference to a series of other groups whose means have been previously found.

Finally, having met all the tests just enumerated, we resort to the probability frame of reference to determine statistical significance when we find that a difference between means is three times its standard error. This is done on the basis of the following procedure. First, we know that the means of many random samples tend to approach the binomial expansion or the normal probability curve, and also that the differences between the means of random samples have the same limit. Second, we can estimate the frequency with which any magnitude of a mean or any difference between means occurs in the fluctuations of random sampling from a homogeneous and infinite universe. Third, when the obtained difference is one whose magnitude can occur very infrequently in random sampling, or only once in 370 trials, we say that the difference is statistically significant, that is, it is a difference which occurs so rarely in the fluctuations of sampling from a homogeneous universe that its occurrence in the present study is *probably* indicative of a real difference between the two groups compared. Note that we cannot

[14] See Appendices A and B.

say it is certainly indicative of a real difference, only that it is probably indicative of a real difference. Finally, although in most cases we deal with an experimental group compared with a control group, both of which are non-random samples and hence do not conform to the strict requirements of random sampling basic to the probability theory, we can at least say that the obtained difference is greater than usually occurs in random sampling, or that it is no greater than might occur in random sampling, as the case may be. The only way in which the probability of the difference being a real one can be generalized to a universe from which the experimental and control groups were chosen is to repeat the experiment and find corroboration on successive trials. Nevertheless the discovery of a significant difference by the operations outlined above is an objective procedure and supplies a degree of confidence that encourages further experimentation under similar conditions. This is its chief positive and constructive value for sociological research.

It should be remembered that the theory of sampling is used to give us a rationale for generalizations from a relatively small group (a sample) to the larger population or universe from which it was chosen. The conditions are: (1) randomization in the selection of the cases in the sample is essential, also the conditions (2) of a large universe (infinite), which is (3) homogeneous in composition. Faced by these conditions both the novice and the purist are inclined to insist that, unless these conditions are met or approximated with reasonable closeness in studies by experimental design, the researcher cannot formulate valid generalizations from the results of his experiment to the population at large.[15] When non-random samples are chosen from a heterogeneous universe, and a limited one at that, as in the case of most of the studies described in this book, doubt is cast upon the results and a lingering sense of intellectual insecurity persists. It is true, of course, that no generalizations to any universe can be made from the results found among the non-

[15] For a more adequate discussion of this problem, see T. C. McCormick, "Note on the Validity of Mathematical Probability in Sociological Research," *American Sociological Review*, October, 1945, pp. 626–631.

random samples in the studies herein described. But then no such claim was anywhere made; we explicitly pointed out in every example that no generalization could be made from any one of these experimental studies *except* with respect to the definitive groups actually studied. We repeatedly stated that the results were limited to the closed system of each particular experiment, and that only replication of the experiment which yielded corroboratory results would supply any reliable basis for generalization to a universe. Since this was the case, of what utility was the use of probability tests on non-random samples?

Rejoinder to this question is simply that the alternative to the use of probability tests would have been to rely on subjectively formed opinions about the importance of the obtained differences or changes in each single experiment even when limited to the definitive groups studied. As was stated earlier, we reject this alternative as unsatisfactory. But suppose the difference between the experimental group and the control group, both being non-random samples, *is* statistically significant; we are then faced with the dilemma as to whether the obtained difference occurred because the two groups were chosen from different universes, or merely because the two samples were non-random. This raises a real difficulty of interpretation. In most cases the experimental group *was made* non-random, either because randomization was not possible, for the practical reasons discussed in pages 168–169, or because the social program or causal factor was brought to bear upon accessible subjects only. In any event, in the present stage of experimental work done in the free community situation we relinquish any argument for generalization that different universes are indicated even when probability tests of the differences between the non-random samples are statistically significant.

In summary, there are four considerations which seem relevant to the use of probability tests on such non-random samples as the experimental and control groups of these experiments.

1. Justification for the use of P-tests in the present provisional state of development of experimental designs in sociological research is essentially pragmatic, as when the over-all results from

the experiment are confirmed by replication,[16] despite the fact that the experimental and control groups are non-randomly selected. The P-tests serve in this context merely as a convenient device to order the data to a rational frame of reference.

2. The result of applying P-tests to non-random samples of the experimental and control groups ". . . at least allows us to say that the observed differences are no greater than might occur with random samples." [17]

3. With respect to the kind of samples, McCormick makes another point: ". . . Because of the difficulties in taking a simple sample under many conditions of sociological research, it is fortunate that the standard errors of simple samples are usually not very different from those of random samples, and in any case are somewhat larger. For these reasons, investigators often apply simple sampling errors to random or even stratified samples, in order to save labor or to be on the conservative side when in doubt as to what the error formula should be." [18]

4. The principle which lies at the basis of P-tests used in the present stage of experimental design in sociological research is: the frequency *distributions of the means* of measures of items in large random samples tend to approach a normal probability distribution, *whatever* may be the distribution of frequencies of measures in the universe; and similarly for the *differences* between the means of random samples. Empirical evidence supporting this principle is widely accepted by statisticians. Moreover, the evidence also tends to approximate even more directly the theoretical model of the binomial expansion. This is a principle which any student may confirm empirically by the tossing of coins, or by placing in a frequency distribution the means of some measured trait of many random samples.

We may now summarize this discussion of the application of

---

[16] It is unfortunately still the fact that replication of experimental design studies in sociological research has yet to take place. Therefore this statement is one of expectation rather than of fact. For further discussion of this point, see footnote 22, p. 78; and pp. 187–189.

[17] T. C. McCormick, *Elementary Social Statistics*, McGraw-Hill, 1941, p. 256.

[18] *Ibid.*, p. 234.

P-tests to random and to non-random samples in the schematic fashion shown in Table 27. To make an application of this scheme, let us take the data of the housing study of Chapter IV, pages 72–73, using the multiple critical ratios for the differences, changes, and

TABLE 27. Schematic Form of Experimental Design for P-Tests

(1)	(2)	(3)	(4)	(5)[a]
1.		Beginning Date T'	Terminal Date T''	Comparisons of Changes
2.	Random sample	$\bar{X}'_R$	$\bar{X}''_R$	$(\bar{X}''_R - \bar{X}'_R) = D$
3. Universe or Population	Control group (non-random)	$\bar{X}'_C$	$\bar{X}''_C$	$(\bar{X}''_C - \bar{X}'_C) = D$
4. F	Experimental group (non-random)	$\bar{X}'_E$	$\bar{X}''_E$	$(\bar{X}''_E - \bar{X}'_E) = 2\ SD+$
5. Comparison of differences		$(\bar{X}'_E - \bar{X}'_C) = 0$	$(\bar{X}''_E - \bar{X}''_C) = 2\ SD+$	
6. Comparison of differences between changes		$[(\bar{X}''_E - \bar{X}'_E) - (\bar{X}''_C - \bar{X}'_C)] = 2\ SD+$		

[a] The heuristic equations in col. (5), expressing changes (D) in the magnitude of means on some measure of effect, should yield a critical ratio of 2 at least in row 4, col. (5), and preferably 3. Similarly the differences in row 5, col. (4); and the differences between changes in row 6, likewise.

It will be noted that these requirements are met in several of the experiments described in this book. See chaps. IV, pp. 70–74, and V, pp. 122–124.

$$\text{Critical ratio} = \frac{(\bar{X}'' - \bar{X}')}{S.D._{(\bar{x}'' - \bar{x}')}}$$

$$\text{Multiple critical ratio} \quad \frac{Cr_1 + Cr_2 + \cdots + Cr_m}{\sqrt{m}}$$

differences in change. The multiple critical ratio obtained for column (3), row 5, is found to be 0.18, which is as it should be if the condition is met that the two groups began the experiment in 1939 essentially similar in respect to the pattern of three measures of the effects of housing. For 1940, the multiple critical ratio *increases* to 1.65, so that although the second condition is not precisely met, it is nevertheless approximated, since the difference in 1940 approaches statistical significance. When, however, the other criteria are checked, the conditions are met. Thus the multiple critical ratio of column (5), row 3, is 1.82, and of column (5), row 4, is 6.01; and the chief criterion of the significance of the comparison, the difference between changes in the experimental group and the control group, yields a multiple critical ratio of 4.97. The reader may also wish to turn to Table 26, page 133, of the rental-tuberculosis study, as another example of the utility of this tabular form as a device to check results.

Although we make no attempt in this book to deal with the detailed mathematical-statistical aspects [19] of the problem created by the application of probability tests to such non-random samples as an experimental and a control group, but attempt merely to state in verbal terms the logic of the problem, it may be helpful to note briefly a semantic confusion which sometimes grows out of an uncritical use of the probability theory, which, if not stated explicitly, tends to embarrass our reasoning rather than to clarify it. Confusion results when an indeterminate and a metaphysical meaning of probability is accepted, and clarification results when an empirical meaning is taken.

Logicians have noted the fact that there are at least two meanings [20] and perhaps three meanings [21] of probability in the literature. Most students of mathematical statistics,[22] and following them the authors of statistical textbooks,[23] *use the empirical meaning of probability as the measure or limit of relative frequency.* It is this latter meaning that has significance for the student of experimental designs and is the meaning used in this book.

[19] M. G. Kendall, *The Advanced Theory of Statistics,* Lippincott, vol. I, 1943.

[20] R. Carnap, "The Two Concepts of Probability," *Philosophical and Phenomenological Research,* June, 1945, pp. 513–532.

[21] E. Nagel, *Principles of the Theory of Probability,* University of Chicago Press, 1939.

[22] Kendall, *op. cit.,* and R. von Mises, *Probability, Statistics, and Truth,* 1928 and 1939.

[23] Margaret J. Hagood, *Statistics for Sociologists,* Reynal & Hitchcock, 1941; see especially pp. 354–369; and T. C. McCormick, *Elementary Social Statistics,* McGraw-Hill, 1941, pp. 234, 256.

The classical conception of probability of Bernoulli and Laplace [24] and of De Morgan,[25] according to which all of our knowledge is regarded as having a probable character, and hence a degree of probability is merely a measure of the amount of certainty associated with belief, is not accepted by Carnap, Nagel, and von Mises. Nor do they accept the meaning of probability as that of a unique logical relation, as used by Keynes [26] and Jeffreys.[27] As to the former, Carnap states, "It must be admitted that the classical Laplacean definition is untenable"; [28] and Nagel holds that it is not clear whether, in this meaning of the concept, probability is regarded as *a measure of belief* (psychological) or as a measure of the degree of belief one *ought* to entertain as reasonable, and finds evidence of circular logic in the Laplacean definition.[29] As to the second conception of probability (Keynes, Jeffreys), Carnap says, "Modern authors, especially Keynes, Jeffreys and Hosiasson [30] have proceeded more cautiously, *but at the price of restricting themselves to axiom systems* which are rather weak and hence far from constituting an explicit definition" [31] (italics ours); and Nagel states, ". . . the conception of probability according to which we cannot in principle control by experiment and observation the probability statements we make is not a conception which recommends itself as germaine to scientific inquiry." [32]

The first two conceptions of probability have been reduced by Carnap to one: the degree of logical confirmation, which he designates as P_1. He states that it is "very important to distinguish clearly between *kinds of events* (war, birth, death, throw of a die, throw of this die, throw of this die yielding an ace, etc.) and *events* (Caesar's death, the throw of a die made yesterday at 10 A.M., the series of all

[24] P. Laplace, *Essai Philosophique sur les Probabilités,* 1814.
[25] A. de Morgan, *An Essay on Probability,* 1838.
[26] J. M. Keynes, *Treatise on Probability,* 1921.
[27] H. Jeffreys, *Scientific Inference,* 1931.
[28] Carnap, *op. cit.,* p. 519.
[29] Nagel, *op. cit.,* p. 46.
[30] J. Hosiasson-Lindenbaum, "On Confirmation," *Journal of Symbolic Logic,* 1940, pp. 133–148.
[31] Carnap, *op. cit.,* p. 520.
[32] Nagel, *op. cit.,* p. 50.

throws of this die past and future)," [33] and continues, "It is clear from probability statement₁, a statement on frequency can never be inferred, because the former is purely logical while the latter is factual. . . ." [34] The second meaning of the concept of probability is empirical—the limit of relative frequency. Of this meaning Kendall says, ". . . The second approach seeks to define probability in terms of the relative frequency of events and thus to throw the theory back to pure mathematics of abstract ensembles (Kolmogoroff, 1933) or to the limiting properties of sequences (von Mises, 1936) . . ."; [35] and again, ". . . a considerable measure of agreement that the concept of probability is founded on our experience of the frequency of observed phenomena . . ." [36] exists among students of the subject. All of which brings us back to the contention that when probability tests are used as illustrated in the studies of this book, *to serve only as an empirical safety device,* and not to provide a basis for extensive generalization, then their use is justified and should help dispel the doubts of the novice and the criticisms of the purist.

A schematic presentation of our analysis appears in Table 28 and shows the kind of referents which seem to stand for the three different meanings of probability. Of the three meanings only the third, row 3, columns (2) and (3), has any fact referent. For this third meaning—probability is the limit of relative frequency—we have at least two kinds of empirical evidence. The one (1), may be obtained by the reader from tossing coins, let us say 6 pennies tossed 64 times, recording after each toss the number of heads up, and then comparing the frequencies with the coefficients of the binomial expansion, $(\frac{1}{2} + \frac{1}{2})^6$. Several such experiments will yield frequencies that will fluctuate in magnitude about the magnitudes of the coefficients of the binomial expansion and, in the long run of many repetitions of the experiment, will approach the binomial expansion as a limit. The other (2), may be obtained by the reader by selecting random samples of uniform size from some reasonably large universe, and then computing the means of some measure

---

[33] Carnap, *op. cit.,* pp. 522–523.
[34] *Ibid.,* p. 526.
[35] Kendall, *op. cit.,* p. 165.
[36] *Ibid.,* pp. 165–166.

and arranging these means in a frequency distribution of seven classes. If several groups of random samples are analyzed in this way and the resulting frequency distributions compared with the coef-

TABLE 28.   Probability and Its Referents [a]

Concept of Term	Referents	
	Having Linguistic Referents (*Designata*)	Having Fact Referents (*Denotata*)
(1)	(2)	(3)

"Probability"	1. A measure of belief
	  (1) degree of belief (intensity)?
	  (2) degree of belief one *ought* to entertain?
		(?)

	2. A unique logical relation which cannot in principle be controlled by observation or experiment	(?)
	3. The measure or limit of relative frequency	(1) Tossing dice or coins many times yields a frequency distribution of attributes which corresponds to the binomial expansion.
	(an operational —→	
	definition) —→	(2) The means of random samples tend to approach the binomial expansion or the probability distribution.

[a] Although this table is similar to Table 1, pp. 23–24, it will be noticed that the order of the second and third main columns is reversed (for logical reasons) in this case.

ficients of the binomial expansion noted above, it will be found that the distribution of the means tends to fluctuate about the binomial and approach it as a limit. In this manner the student may perform certain operations and obtain confirmation of the definition of probability as the limit of relative frequency.[37]

[37] For a more adequate discussion, see Hagood, *op. cit.*, pp. 354–358, 366.

The Null Hypothesis Again

Our earlier discussion of the advantages in sociological research of the null hypothesis (Chapter IV, pp. 70–74) need not be repeated here, but it may be worth while nevertheless to note that the use of probability tests [38] is facilitated by the null hypothesis, since the relevant evidence to support or to refute this hypothesis is based, in part at least, upon the relative frequency of occurrence of various magnitudes of difference or of change. In the closed system of a single experiment the null hypothesis is particularly helpful. The positive type of hypothesis in sociological research usually posits "improvement," or "change" in a desired direction, and is thus an open-ended statement, one which has an indefinite end approached only by an infinite number of small increments, and an end that often recedes as it is approached (the higher the standard of living goes, the more ways there are of being poor!). An open-ended system of effects is difficult to handle empirically. But the null hypothesis, by comparison, provides a closed system. Departures from an arbitrarily fixed zero point can be measured.

OBSTACLES TO REPLICATION

Confirmation of the results of tests of some program by experimental design is the criterion [39] we have set up as the goal of ex-

---

[38] For further discussion of the null hypothesis see Hagood, *op. cit.*, and Lindquist, *op. cit.*, pp. 15–16, where he remarks, "In many sampling studies the interest is not so much in the limits within which a parameter may confidently be said to be, as in the single possibility that the parameter is zero . . . such hypotheses —that the parameter is zero—are known as null hypotheses. If a statistic is such that the null hypothesis may be rejected with confidence, we say that the statistic is significant, meaning that it signifies that the parameter value is not zero . . . however . . . to prove the difference significant does not establish the cause of the difference. . . ."

[39] Says Alfred J. Ayer, "The criterion which we use to test the genuineness of apparent statements of fact is the criterion of verifiability. We say that a sentence is factually significant to any given person, if, and only if, he knows how to verify the proposition which it purports to express—that is, if he knows what observations would lead him, under certain conditions, to accept the proposition as being true, or reject it as being false. . . ." *Language, Truth and Logic,* Oxford, 1936, pp. 19–20.

perimental study. Why is repetition of the experimental test of a hypothesis so infrequent in sociological research?

There seem to be several explanations of this state of affairs. Experimental designs are new and strange. They run counter to certain established predilections which are current in social research. In fact, it was as recent as 1932 that many sociologists asserted that there never could be any experimental study of human relations.[40] Philosophical controversies about the meaning of the concept "cause and effect," together with the ethical complexities of the means-ends schema, effectively combined to confuse discussion of experimental designs in sociological research. Existent results of crude experimental study were often indecisive and hence seemed additional substantiation of the claims of its critics. Some students may have been reluctant to undertake systematic and planned research that required thorough analysis and the use of measurement devices. The expense of an experimental study may also have been a deterrent. In connection with this last point it may be of interest that the fairly extensive studies of morale and relief of Chapter III, pages 41–50, and of the social effects of public housing, Chapter IV, pages 58–79, cost in each case the sum of approximately $2000 to complete, from planning through publication, and including supervision.

Now that many standardized sociometric scales are available for social observation and measurement, and a variety of exploratory efforts at experimental study have defined the patterns of the projected and the ex post facto experimental designs, it would seem that the situation in sociological research is ready for repetition of some of the pioneering studies. The fact that these investigations were far

[40] Robert C. Angell, "The Difficulties of Experimental Sociology," *Social Forces,* vol. XI, No. 2, December, 1932, pp. 207–210, lists the difficulties as recognized in 1932. In general, confusion of thought about experimental sociology stems from failure to distinguish between: (a) experiments in social reform by the method of trial and error, which inevitably include *restraints* on certain individual freedoms; and (b) experimental design study that makes observations of human relations under conditions which control some of the variable factors, not by interference with individual freedoms, but by matching the measurements of several factors. See also, H. C. Brearley, "Experimental Sociology in the United States," *Social Forces,* December, 1931.

from perfect experimental designs is no excuse for the failure to try to repeat them. A recent study of public housing in Newark [41] made during 1942 and 1943 did not utilize the standardized sociometric scales which had been used in the Minneapolis study described in Chapter IV, although the results of this Minneapolis study had been published in December of 1940.[42] If the techniques of experimental study of the problems of human relations are to be made more reliable and precise, they should be tried out again and again. Repetition in the use of such tools of social observation as many of the sociometric scales described in Chapter VI has led to great improvement in some of these devices. It remains for the student of human relations to repeat also in the use of experimental designs for sociological study.

The Value of a Verification of Values

John Dewey contends that "operational thinking needs to be applied to the judgment of values just as it has now finally been applied in conceptions of physical objects. Experimental empiricism in the field of ideas of good and bad is demanded to meet the conditions of the present situation." [43] And again, ". . . carrying over experimental method from physics to man concerns the import of standards, principles, rules." "They (the rules) would lose all pretense of formality. . . . The change would do away with the intolerance and fanaticism that attend the notion that beliefs and judgments are capable of inherent truth and authority." ". . . Any

[41] J. Rumney and S. Shuman, *The Social Effects of Public Housing in Newark, N. J.,* Housing Authority of the City of Newark, November, 1944, 95 pp.; 2nd printing, March, 1946. The authors state on p. 2, "It was possible for us to match the two groups only on the basis of certain general characteristics," but do not make clear to the reader what these factors are. There is some internal evidence in the report that the factors age, sex, and race were used (pp. 24–25, 28–29, 32), and yet when the published tables are examined it is evident that race (Negro, white) was far from equalized in comparisons. Furthermore, the authors state (pp. 38, 43, 46, 69) that the obtained differences were not statistically significant but do not inform the reader as to exactly what the differences or critical ratios were, nor whether the criterion was the 2-per-cent or the 1-per-cent level. See also, for comment on this study, chap. IV, footnote 22.

[42] *American Sociological Review,* December, 1940, pp. 868–879.

[43] *The Quest for Certainty,* Minton, Balch & Co., 1929.

belief as such is tentative, hypothetical." "A moral law . . . its soundness and pertinence are tested by what happens when it is acted upon," and again, "The test of consequences is more exacting than that afforded by fixed general rules." [44]

These are encouraging words and stimulating ideas. It hardly seems necessary to point out that the experimental studies described in this book (except the tuberculosis study of Chapter V) are tests of the efficacy of specific means to attain desired ends; in short, they are examples of operational thinking about social values. This is particularly the case for the six studies which concern adjustment as an end to be achieved by such means as programs of public housing (pp. 41–50), social treatment of juvenile delinquency (pp. 84–91, 97–99), and formal classroom education for the masses (pp. 99–124) or avocational counseling of individual students (pp. 79–93). Is it too much to hope that experimental designs in sociological research as exemplified in these pioneering studies may have blazed the trail that will enable the student of human relations to accomplish two much-to-be-desired goals: first, to appraise by scientific methods of research the effectiveness of specific means to achieve certain ends; and second, to be able to isolate cause-and-effect relationships in the complicated area of human relations?

[44] *Ibid.*, pp. 277–278.

Appendix A

REVISED TENTATIVE NORMS—SOCIAL STATUS SCALE SCORES (1942)

1. Previous norms (1933) suggested for interpretation of scores:

Class	Ranges in Scores	
Upper middle	125–149	
Average middle	100–124	See p. 378, F. Stuart
Lower middle	75–99	Chapin, *Contempo-*
Workingmen's homes	50–74	*rary American Institu-*
Relief, poverty	25–49	*tions,* Harper &
Destitute	0–24	Brothers, 1935

2. Since the depression of the thirties, several studies have shown a trend to higher scores for families receiving relief and on work relief. Also, studies by George A. Lundberg have shown ranges in score on the homes of normal families living in a New England village. Study of results procured in different parts of the country suggests a revision of the class categories to correspond to higher social status scores as follows:

3. Revised tentative norms applicable in 1942 (after Lundberg):

Class		Ranges in Scores	Examples
Upper:	1. Upper part	250 and over	Professional, physician
	2. Lower part	200–249	Small town banker
Middle:	1. Upper part	150–199	Factory manager
	2. Lower part	100–149	Skilled trades
Lower:	1. Upper part	50–99	Unemployed semi-skilled
	2. Lower part	0–49	Unemployed unskilled

4. Some recent studies which supply new data:

George A. Lundberg, "The Measurement of Socioeconomic Status," *American Sociological Review,* February, 1940, pp. 29–39.

G. A. Lundberg and Margaret Lansing, "The Sociography of Some Community Relations," *ibid.,* June, 1937, pp. 318–335.

G. A. Lundberg and Mary Steele, "Social Attraction Patterns in a Village," *Sociometry,* January-April, 1938, pp. 375–419.

Louis Guttman, "A Revision of Chapin's Social Status Scale," *American Sociological Review,* June, 1942, pp. 362–369.

(These weights were not used in Tables 1 and 3 above.)

5. Distributions of scores from representative samples of urban populations:

(1) Total social status score: approaches a normal or symmetrical distribution, 0 to over 220 points; slightly skewed to higher scores; modal scores 80 to 135.

(2) Score on part II, condition of the living room, a J-curve; skewed to lower scores − 16 to − 10; mode at + 8.

MEASUREMENT OF CONDITION OF THE LIVING ROOM OF A DWELLING

Part II: Condition of Articles in Living Room

To provide some objective rating of qualitative attributes of the living room, such as "aesthetic atmosphere" or "general impression," the following additional items may be noted. The visitor should check the words that seem to describe the situation. Some of the weights are of minus sign, and so operate as penalties to reduce the total score of the home.

18. Cleanliness of room and furnishings

    a. Spotted or stained (−4)................................____

    b. Dusty (−2)..____

    c. Spotless and dustless (+2)..........................____

19. Orderliness of room and furnishings

    a. Articles strewn about in disorder (−2)...............____

    b. Articles in place or in usable order (+2)..............____

20. Condition of repair of articles and furnishings

    a. Broken, scratched, frayed, ripped, or torn (−4)..........——

    b. Articles or furnishings patched up (−2)...............——

    c. Articles or furnishings in good repair and well kept (+2).——

21. Record your general impression of good taste

    a. Bizarre, clashing, inharmonious, or offensive (−4)......——

    b. Drab, monotonous, neutral, inoffensive (−2)...........——

    c. Attractive in a positive way, harmonious, quiet and restful

    (+2)..——

    Score on Part II....——   Total score,[a] Parts I and II....——

[a] The entire scale, Parts I and II, was published in F. Stuart Chapin, *Contemporary American Institutions*, Harper & Brothers, 1935, and W. C. Brown (Dubuque), 1946, pp. 373–397. Penalties for use-crowding on total score of parts I and II are: (1) use of living room also as a dining room, deduct 6 points; (2) used also as a kitchen, deduct 9; (3) used also as a bedroom, *or* as a dining room and kitchen combined, deduct 12; (4) used also as a bedroom, dining room, and kitchen combined, deduct 15.

CHAPIN'S SOCIAL STATUS SCALE WITH THE NEW WEIGHTS COMPUTED BY LOUIS GUTTMAN [1]

PART I. MATERIAL EQUIPMENT AND CULTURAL EXPRESSION OF THE LIVING ROOM OF THE HOME

	Old Weights	New Weights
1. Floor, softwood	6	8.4
hardwood	10	13.9
2. Large rug	8	5.6
3. Windows with drapes	each 2	each 3.6
4. Fireplace with 3 or more utensils	8	34.3
5. Artificial light, electric	8	12.0
kerosene	− 2	− 3.0
6. Library table	8	− 1.0
7. Armchairs	each 8	each 4.1
8. Piano bench	4	5.2
9. Desk: personal-social	8	2.3

[1] See 4. Revised Tentative Norms—Social Status Scale Scores (1942).

	Old Weights	New Weights
10. Bookcases with books	each 8	each 3.4
11. Sewing machine	— 2	2.0
12. Couch pillows	each 2	each .7
13. Alarm clock	— 2	— 5.3
14. Periodicals	each 8	each 1.6
15. Newspapers	each 8	each 7.7
16. Telephone	8	24.4
17. Radio	8	8.0

PART II. CONDITION OF ARTICLES IN LIVING ROOM

18. Cleanliness of room and furnishings		
a. Spotted or stained	— 4	— 19.4
b. Dusty	— 2	— 9.7
c. Spotless and dustless	2	9.7
19. Orderliness of room and furnishings		
a. Articles strewn about in disorder	— 2	— 19.7
b. Articles in place or in usable order	2	19.7
20. Condition of repair of articles and furnishings		
a. Broken, scratched, frayed, ripped, or torn	— 4	— 16.3
b. Articles or furnishings patched up	— 2	— 8.1
c. Articles or furnishings in good repair and well kept	2	8.1
21. Record your general impression of good taste		
a. Bizarre, clashing, inharmonious, or offensive	— 4	— 5.4
b. Drab, monotonous, neutral, inoffensive	— 2	— 2.7
c. Attractive in a positive way, harmonious, quiet and restful	2	2.7

TENTATIVE NORMS OF SOCIAL PARTICIPATION SCALE

SOCIAL PARTICIPATION SCALE —
TENTATIVE NORMS (1944)

Occupational Groups	N	Mean Social Participation Scores		Range
I. Professional and business leaders	22	1. Top business and professions	(65)	46–65
	26	2. Top civic leaders	(51)	
	17	3. Emergent leaders [a]	(46)	
	24	4. Top U-student leaders	(56)	
II. Semi-professional and managerial	18	5. Proprietary and managerial	(26)	26–32
	12	6. Labor leaders	(28)	
III. Clerical workers	46	7. Clerical workers	(16)	14–16
IV. Skilled workers	10	8. Skilled workers	(10)	8–15
V. Semi-skilled	4	9. Semi-skilled workers		13–15
Unemployed, Relief	44	10. Slum population		8
	44	11. Relief clients		5
Random Sample	233	12. Random sample [b] of population (includes Nos. 3 and 6)		10

[a] A group of natural leaders of the community who emerged from a survey on a representative urban sample: F. Stuart Chapin, *Community Leadership and Opinion in Red Wing,* University of Minnesota Press, 1945, 26 pp., especially pp. 6, 23.
[b] *Ibid.,* p. 24.

SOCIAL PARTICIPATION SCALE

HUSBAND

Case No............

Address............

Age............ Education............ Race or Nationality............

Occupation............ Income............

Name of Organization	1. Member [a]	2. Attendance	3. Financial Contributions	4. Member of Committees (Not Name)	5. Offices Held
1					
2					
3					
4					
5					
6					
7					
8					
9					
10					
Totals............					

WIFE

Age.................................... Education.................................... Race or Nationality....................................

Occupation.................................... Income....................................

Name of Organization	1. Member [a]	2. Attendance	3. Financial Contributions	4. Member of Committees (Not Name)	5. Offices Held
1					
2					
3					
4					
5					
6					
7					
8					
9					
10					
Totals....................................					

Date.................................... Investigator....................................

[a] Enter L if purely local group; enter N if a local unit of a state or national organization.

Distribution of total scores from a representative sample of an urban population, a J-curve; skewed to higher scores of 100 and over; mode at 0 to 11 points.

AUTHOR'S INDEX

Alpert, H., 155
Anderson, J. E., 152
Anderson, W. A., 157
Angell, R. C., 188
Arkin, H., 122
Arrington, R. E., 149, 157
Ayer, A. J., 187

Barer, N., viii, x, 97
Barr, F. E., 114, 152, 157
Bell, H. M., 36, 37, 38
Bellows, M. T., 126
Bernard, J., 150, 151, 157, 161
Bernoulli, 184
Black, B. J., 78
Blumer, H., 155
Bogardus, E. S., 150, 157
Bowers, R. V., 154
Brearley, H. C., 188
Britten, R., 128
Burdick, E. M., 152, 157
Burrus, J. N., viii, 95, 124

Carnap, R., 135, 159, 183, 184
Carter, H., 144
Chapin, C. V., 146, 157
Chapin, F. S., 22, 36, 39, 48, 49, 63–
    65, 92, 95, 109, 143, 149–155, 157,
    161, 162, 165, 192, 193, 195
Chapin, H. D., 5
Chapman, J. C., 152, 157
Christiansen, H., viii, 99, 100, 101,
    104, 105, 107, 108, 111, 172
Clark, W. W., 147
Colton, R. C., 122
Commons, J. R., 152, 157

Comte, A., 1, 2
Cottam, H., 153

Dashiell, W. N., 146
Davidson, D., Jr., 149
De Morgan, A., 184
Dewey, J., 189
Dodd, S. C., viii, x, 55–57, 150, 155,
    157
Droba, D. D., 144
Drolet, G. J., 126
Dublin, L. I., 16
Dunham, H. W., 144

Elmer, M. C., 146, 147, 157
Engel, F., 152, 157
Ezekiel, M., 35, 111

Feldstein, J. J., 149
Fisher, R. A., 31, 42, 46
Fourier, C., 7, 10, 11, 12
Frame, N., 146, 157
Frank, L. C., 146
Franz, J. G., 149, 157
Frost, W. G., 4
Fuchs, A. W., 146

Garrett, H. E., 107
Goode, H., 126
Goodenough, F., 152, 157
Goodenough, W. H., 150, 160
Green, H. W., 129
Greenwood, E., ix, 95, 129
Gross, L., 151, 157
Guilford, J. P., 81, 82
Guttman, L., 42, 108–110, 122, 150,
    157, 160, 162, 163, 172, 192, 193

199

SUBJECT INDEX

203